MICHAEL DEWAR

Defence of the Nation

ARMS AND
ARMOUR

To Lavinia, Alexander, James, Edward and Katharine

First published in Great Britain in 1989 by Arms and Armour Press, Artillery House, Artillery Row, London SW1P 1RT.

Distributed in the USA by Sterling Publishing Co. Inc., 387 Park Avenue South, New York, NY 10016 8810.

Distributed in Australia by Capricorn Link (Australia) Pty. Ltd., P.O. Box 665, Lane Cove, New South Wales 2066, Australia.

British Library Cataloguing in Publication Data
Dewar, Michael
Defence of the nation.
1. Great Britain. Defence. Policies of government
I. Title
355′.0335′41
ISBN 0 85368 836 2

Designed and edited by DAG Publications Ltd. Designed by David Gibbons; edited by Michael Boxall; layout by Anthony A. Evans; typeset by Typesetters (Birmingham) Ltd.; camerawork by M&E Reproductions, North Fambridge, Essex; printed and bound in Great Britain by Richard Clay Ltd, Bungay, Suffolk

Contents

Introduction

While I was taking part in Exercise 'Brave Defender' in September 1985, the largest Home Defence Exercise to take place since the Second World War, it struck me how few of my civilian friends understood the complexity and scope of the plans which we were putting into practice. Yet it concerned them all. I undertook some research to establish just how much and what had been written about Home Defence. I discovered a host of somewhat esoteric books written mostly by academics on the nuclear holocaust but little about Home Defence, and certainly nothing by a serving soldier who might know a little about the subject. There were books with chapter titles such as 'The impact of latent nuclear war on democracy'. Most assumed that an attack on Britain would be nuclear and paid little or no heed to the conventional defence of these islands.

Beneath the City Streets by Peter Laurie was first published in 1979 and a revised and updated edition was published in 1983. It is subtitled 'A Private Enquiry into Government Preparations for National Emergency'. Chapter 2 of the book headed 'What the H bomb does to people, houses and other things', assumes that the Third World War will be nuclear from the outset. *War Plan UK* by Duncan Campbell was first published in 1982 and has since been published in paperback. Campbell's approach is more historical and he looks at the effects of war on civilians in Britain 1914–49 and Home Defence in the nuclear age 1949–72. He then jumps straight into a detailed study of the effects of nuclear bombs on Britain. In his *The Unsinkable Aircraft Carrier*, subtitled 'American military Power in Britain', first published in 1984, the emphasis is again, though less so, on the nuclear role of US Forces in Britain.

These books and many more like them adopt a simplistic approach to what in reality is a much more complex and involved subject. In fact we cannot assume that a future conflict in Europe will 'go nuclear' or, if it does, that it will go nuclear quickly. The Soviet Union's overwhelming conventional capability (and the Russians regard chemical weapons as 'conventional') over NATO means that the Russians are unlikely to initiate nuclear warfare if they can achieve their aim conventionally. Whether in reality NATO would be prepared to start a nuclear war is an open question. Certainly NATO strategy on the Central Front is to maintain conventional operations as long as possible, if feasible indefinitely. It is becoming more and more evident that the use of nuclear weapons could lead to mutual destruction. Today's massive nuclear stock pile is therefore increasingly being called into question. Both the INF Treaty and START negotiations bear witness to this trend.

In the conventional weapon sector the armed forces of the NATO powers are quantitively inferior to those of the Warsaw Pact nations by a factor of approximately 3 to 1. As things stand, recourse to nuclear weapons by NATO inside a relatively short period of time would seem almost inevitable. General Bernard Rogers, who retired as Supreme Allied Commander, Europe (SACEUR) in 1987, stated shortly before his retirement that he would have been obliged, within just a few days of war breaking out, to request authorization to use nuclear weapons. As a result of this and other warnings NATO has therefore agreed certain measures to reinforce the conventional defensive capability of the Alliance. The FOFA (Follow on Forces Attack) concept, proposed by General Rogers, was adopted on 9 November 1984 by NATO's Defence Planning Committee to provide the basis for the long term planning for the defence of Europe. The objective of FOFA is to weaken the combat forces of the enemy's second strategic echelon before they arrive at the front line and before they have deployed into less vulnerable battle formations. Air and missile attacks would be carried out on concentrated targets in the rear areas and along the lines of communication, thus preventing a breakthrough into western Europe by Russian forces. By isolating and destroying these second echelon forces it would be much easier to contain and defeat Russian first echelon formations by mobile counter-attack operations which would aim to restore the integrity of NATO borders. These counter attacks would be carried out by armoured formations supported by artillery, attack helicopters and offensive aircraft. The main battle tank would therefore remain the main weapons system of NATO land forces for the forseeable future.

Increased urbanization and deforestation in the Central European theatre means an attacker can only concentrate a certain percentage of his available forces in the first attack wave. FOFA would therefore aim to prevent the enemy from reinforcing the success of his leading formations. Without going into the finer details of FOFA, which is not the purpose of this book, suffice it to say that NATO strategists are trying to ensure at least a longer if not an indefinite conventional phase. To assume that an attack on the United Kingdom would be nuclear, which has been the tendency in many commentaries on the subject, is therefore becoming increasingly wide of the mark. There is a certain need to plan for the conventional defence of the United Kingdom while at the same time recognizing the possibility that a conflict in Europe could go nuclear. Current arms control negotiations can only reinforce this trend.

Where does Britain fit into all of this? The fact is that the geographical location of the British Isles means that Britain must inevitably play a central role in any future conflict. NATO naval operations in the eastern Atlantic and in the strategically important UK Iceland Gap would be controlled from headquarters in the United Kingdom. British and US nuclear submarines would sail from bases in this country. US and British reinforcements for the Central Front would sail from British ports or fly from British airfields. Much of the command communications and logistic back up for British forces in Germany, Belgium, Denmark and Norway is located in this country. And of course a large number of US and British Strike Aircraft are based at airfields in East Anglia and central England. Together these land, sea and air forces make up a substantial part of NATO's total capability. The Soviet Union would be unlikely to ignore Britain's central role in NATO. It follows that Britain must plan an adequate defence of the homeland in order to protect it against attack and provide a secure base from which it can carry out its NATO role.

Although the conventional defences of the United Kingdom are little publicized, a highly sophisticated 'layered' system of defences has existed for some time, exists today and is constantly being updated and improved. It is the purpose of this book to explain the conventional defences of this island to the layman. This has not been attempted before and it is high time it was done.

1. The History of Home Defence

The last successful invasion of Britain was in 1066. Considering the leading role which Britain has played on the world stage since that date it is perhaps surprising that there has not been a successful attempt at invasion during this period by one or another of her enemies. It is even more surprising when one realizes just how many attempts have been mounted against the British Isles.

Before 1066 invasions were either part of a larger scheme or part of a migratory pattern. They did not happen because Britain posed a threat. Caesar's incursions in 55 54BC and Claudius's more permanent occupation of the island in AD43 were arbitrary extensions of the 'Pax Romana'; the Saxons in 449, the Angles in 547 and the successive waves of Danes from the eighth to the eleventh centuries all represented a migratory phenomenon. The Norman Conquest in 1066 came about as a result of a dynastic dispute and, as we all know, it was spectacularly successful. But extraordinarily it was never repeated.

During the Middle Ages, even if a foreign force managed to set foot on English soil, it was always quickly driven out again. This happened with a Danish raid in 1135, then again in 1359 when a party of French seamen sacked Winchelsea as well as in 1377 when the French succeeded in sacking Portsmouth after landing on the Isle of Wight. But all these affairs were more in the nature of raids. It was not until the end of the sixteenth century that England again faced the threat of invasion. Exactly what led Philip II of Spain to launch the Armada against England in 1588 is still a matter of some dispute among historians. One thing is certain, however: England was fast becoming a threat to Spain's monopoly of power and wealth in the Americas. Even though it may have been the execution of Mary Queen of Scots by Queen Elizabeth that was the immediate cause of Philip's decision to send a mighty fleet against England, the deeper and more abiding reason was that English privateers were now actively challenging Spanish power in the Americas.

It is not the purpose of this book to recount the story of the defeat of the Armada in 1588.[1] In any event the story is well known. What is not so well known is that Spain had not yet done with Elizabeth. In 1601 forty ships and 5,000 troops sailed for the Irish coast. Once again they were battered by the wind and the waves and some of the ships were forced to turn for home. Three thousand men landed at Kinsale in September 1601 to bolster Irish rebels, but it was too little and too late. The Spanish invaders were finally forced to surrender on 2 January 1602 and the rebellion was crushed.

British foreign policy under the Stuarts was to remain friendly with both France and Spain; consequently the British Isles enjoyed a century free from the threat of invasion. But with the succession of the Protestant William of Orange to the English throne in 1688 and the flight of James II and his family into exile in France, Britain was again under threat from France. Louis XIV was able to land an army in Ireland unopposed in support of the Jacobite cause. It was defeated by William at the Boyne in 1690. In retaliation the French launched a five hour raid on Teignmouth in 1692. Although it was a fairly pointless exercise in plunder and looting, it proved to the French that it was possible to make a landfall on English soil.

The Jacobite threat to William became increasingly serious. In 1708 the Stuart Pretender got as far as the coast of Scotland. In 1715 he landed in Scotland without foreign aid and instigated the rising of that year. In 1719 a Spanish army actually made a landfall in Scotland. And in 1745 there were French troops in Prince Charles Edward Stuart's army. Meanwhile another French army lay in the ports of Picardy ready to strike across the Channel. The Jacobite threat was finally ended on the field of Culloden in 1746.

War again broke out with France in 1756. Louis XV soon appreciated that French Canada was slowly being brought to its knees by the stranglehold that the Royal Navy held on the Atlantic sea lanes. Once again the only really effective way of striking back at England was invasion. In July 1756 50,000 French troops were brought together in encampments at La Hogue, St Malo, Dunkirk, Calais, Dieppe, Le Havre, Granville and St-Valéry. But a diversionary attack on the British base in Minorca failed to draw the British fleet away from the Channel and the attempt was abandoned. Not to be put out by this setback, the Duc de Choiseul – now the Foreign Minister – began assembling a fleet of 337 flat bottomed boats in Le Havre that would take an army of 48,000 troops to the south coast of England. A second army of 20,000 men would be landed in Scotland to take Edinburgh and a third army of 40,000 men would be transported from Ostend to land at Maldon in Essex. Again it would be necessary either to defeat or divert the British fleet. Any hope of this precondition ever being achieved was quickly ended when the British fleet under Admiral Hawke vanquished the French battle fleet at Quiberon Bay on 20 November 1759. This was one of the decisive sea battles in British naval history. After the battle the French Navy was finished as a credible fighting force.

One can only admire French persistence. By 1779 they were at it again. Vergennes, who was Foreign Minister, had enlisted Spanish help in a scheme which involved two aims: a major naval victory in the Channel and the capture of Portsmouth. Vergennes calculated that both aims were feasible. Many Royal Navy ships of the line were overseas, particularly in America fighting the colonists, and he calculated that the Franco Spanish fleet could gain a local superiority. The fall of Portsmouth would be a major blow to England, cause financial panic in London and could even lead to general bankruptcy.

A Franco Spanish fleet of some 70 ships was assembled off Portugal in June. But even at this stage it had been attacked by a variety of maladies: scurvy, seasickness, smallpox and putrid fever. The Spanish were six weeks late at the rendezvous point and morale was already low. When favourable winds finally blew this second Armada into the Channel in early August, they were faced by an inferior English fleet under Sir Charles Hardy. The weather then intervened and the two fleets managed to sail unseen past each other more than once during August. When they finally came in sight of each other on 31 August, Hardy's ships sheered off hoping to draw the French and Spanish vessels further up the Channel and farther away from reinforcements and provisions at Brest. It worked. Finally it was all too much for the invaders: a combination of the effects of sickness, shortage of water and provisions and disagreements between the Spanish and French finally led them to abandon the entire project. The hundred or so ships that limped into Brest in mid September were little more than floating hospitals.

There were one or two sporadic French attempts against England during the Revolutionary era but, by and large, France was too bound up in her own internal affairs to bother about the traditional enemy until Napoleon Bonaparte began serious preparations for invasion in 1801. By October 1803 the French Minister of Marine, Decrès, was able to report that an invasion flotilla of 1,367 vessels of all types had been assembled, most of them at Boulogne. By October Bonaparte had established his headquarters just outside Boulogne. There were to be 76,798 infantry, 11,640 cavalry, 3,790 gunners and approximately 20,000 supporting troops and non combatants involved in the enterprise against England. In England the threat was being taken very seriously indeed: three main battle fleets were deployed for England's defence. Admiral Cornwallis, in command of the Channel Fleet, patrolled the area from Rochefort to Brest. Admiral Lord Keith, Commander of the English coast between the Downs and Selsey Bill, had to safeguard the North Sea as well as act as back up to the Channel Fleet. And in the Mediterranean England's greatest naval hero, Admiral Lord Nelson, threatened France from the south. On land huge numbers of volunteers had been raised while on the coast fire beacons reminiscent of 1588 were readied to signal the approach of the French flotilla.

But by the end of 1803 the French preparations had come to nothing. The flotilla had proved too unseaworthy for a winter crossing. The business of moving shipping from peripheral ports to the concentration area was not only proving to be a logistic nightmare but was also subject to English attack. Tides and the weather, moreover, made the whole enterprise marginal, particularly in view of the British superiority in men of war. Napoleon did not finally abandon his plans for an invasion until August 1805 when he received the news that Admiral Villeneuve with 35 ships of the line had allowed himself to be bottled up in Cadiz by just three British warships. He disbanded the camp at Boulogne and the Army of England marched away to fight the Austrians. On 21 October Horatio Nelson secured British supremacy of the sea at Trafalgar.

Although it is possible to categorize various locally or privately raised bands of volunteers as 'Home Guards' or 'Home Defence volunteers' at almost any stage during the history of our island, whether they were raised to meet the threat of invasion by Duke William of Normandy in 1066 or that of the Spanish Armada in 1588 or of Napoleon I for some years either side of 1800, a properly constituted home defence force – as opposed to a standing army involved in home defence duties – did not really come into existence until 1860. Victorian Britain was afflicted by a chronic anxiety about invasion. The fear that the British coastline lay open to a French landing was rarely absent from the minds of responsible statesmen.

The anxiety about invasion first became a matter of political importance in 1844 after the publication of a pamphlet by the Prince de Joinville, son of Louis Philippe, in which was outlined the possibility of a French steam navy inflicting heavy losses on British coasts. The publicity given to this pamphlet was followed quickly by a crisis in Franco British relations caused by clashes of interests in Tahiti and Morocco. War was mentioned openly as a possibility and from that time onwards the Prime Minister, Peel, was very much aware of the defences of the country – or the lack of them. Despite all the talk, however, little in practice was done and it was not until Louis Napoleon's *coup* of 2 December 1851, that the invasion scare revived. The Militia Bill, empowering the government to raise a force of up to 120,000 men in cases of great national emergency, was passed by Parliament the following year and then the Crimean War, in which the French and British fought as allies against Russia, intervened. But in the late 1850s there was again cause for real alarm. During the Crimean War French ironclad floating batteries had proved themselves extremely effective against Russian shells. Britain was much slower to put her faith in ironclads, and by 1858 there was deep rooted concern that the French technological lead was positively dangerous to the security of the country.

In these circumstances the slightest sign of hostility from the French was likely to turn concern into something approaching panic. From 1858 there were a succession of such signs. There was the development of the port of Cherbourg for which the British could see no other use than as a port of embarkation for an attack on Britain. There was the indignant French reaction to the fact that the bomb thrown by Orsini at Napoleon III had been made in England. There was the constant fear that France was seeking an alliance with her Crimean enemy, Russia, an alliance which the British saw as directed against themselves. And finally there was suspicion about Napoleon's motives in his intervention in Italy, a suspicion which was apparently justified in 1860 with the annexation of Savoy and Nice.

The panic was initially focused on the inadequacies of the navy, and in 1859 substantial extra funds were voted in Parliament to finance a new naval building programme. At the same time the construction of additional coastal fortifications was undertaken. But it was not so much the government as a handful of interested enthusiasts who saw safety in yet a third remedy, the creation of a Volunteer Rifle Corps. There was historical precedent for this. At times of crisis during the eighteenth century, particularly during the French Revolutionary and Napoleonic wars, the government had been glad to accept offers of service from volunteers.

Government authorization for the Volunteer Force, as it was to be known, was contained in a government circular to Lords Lieutenant of counties on 12 May 1859. The Force was to be raised under the provisions of an existing Act of Parliament, that of 1804, which had consolidated all previous Acts relating to volunteer forces. The circular stated that the Force was 'liable to be called out in case of actual invasion or appearance of an enemy in force on the coast or in case of a rebellion arising out of either of these emergencies'. Estimates vary as to the initial size of the Volunteer Force, but it is thought to have been more than 100,000 strong. Certainly on 23 June 1860 21,000 of its members paraded in Hyde Park in front of the Queen. They were there of their own free will and they trained and clothed themselves at their own expense.

During the first ten years of its existence the Volunteer Force underwent a remarkable transformation. Originally envisaged as a military institution for the middle class, it became largely working class. As government financial aid increased, so also did government insistence on a greater approximation to Regular Army notions of military life. The Force settled down during the 1870s as an accepted institution with a strength of about 200,000. However many critics were doubtful whether the Volunteers, with their relative lack of discipline and training, could play any useful role in preventing or defeating the invasion which the Victorians so feared. Nevertheless, home defence remained the justification for the continued existence of the Force up until the turn of the century when the Boer War led to a searching examination of Britain's military organization, an examination which was to continue until the outbreak of war in 1914. In 1905, talks were initiated with the French Government which were to commit the British Army to fighting on the continent of Europe in alliance with the French. R. B. Haldane, who had just been appointed Secretary of State for War, now had to provide what came to be called an Expeditionary Force, the most probable area of service of which would be Europe, and he also had to ensure that there would be forces left in Britain which would be large enough and efficient enough not only to repel raids but also to provide the necessary reserves for the expeditionary force. Haldane's predecessors had considered the Volunteer Force incapable of this latter role.

So it was that on 4 March 1907 Haldane introduced his Territorial and Reserve Forces Bill in the House of Commons. This created the Territorial Army which was to incorporate the old Volunteer Force. The Territorial Army was to be administered by local Associations. To this end Haldane targeted the Lords Lieutenant of counties through no lesser person than the King. On 26 October 1907 Lords Lieutenant were invited to Buckingham Palace where their support was enlisted. The Volunteer Force ceased to exist on 1 April 1908 and was replaced by the very similar Territorial Army. Although a minority of the new force accepted the liability to serve overseas, it remained what the Volunteers had been, primarily a force for home defence.

The Volunteer Force enjoyed a brief renaissance from 1916 to 1919 when Commands were encouraged to recruit volunteer battalions specifically for home defence purposes, the Territorial Army now being mostly concerned with supplying battalions to serve in France. The Coastal Artillery branch of the Royal Artillery also flourished, the Coast Artillery School at Golden Hill on the Isle of Wight having some fifty officers under instruction at any one time.

The Territorial Army continued to be the focus for home defence matters throughout the inter war years though, once again, as it became involved with the possibility of service overseas after 1940, the need arose for an additional force for home defence. The Local Defence Volunteers (or LDV as they were known) were virtually raised overnight. After only three days of discussion and planning at the War Office and at GHQ Home Forces, the Secretary of State for War broadcast an appeal for volunteers on the evening of 14 May 1940. Even as the broadcast continued the first volunteers arrived at their local police stations to enrol and for the next two days harassed desk sergeants recorded names. Lords Lieutenant of counties were confirmed in their age old responsibilities for raising forces in an emergency by a telegram

Below: Volunteer taking the loyal oath during the First World War. After 1916 the Volunteer Force raised specifically for Home Defence purposes enjoyed a brief renaissance. It was replaced by the Territorial Army.

from the Secretary of State, and Area Commanders of Home Forces were charged with detailed planning. Counties were divided into areas of suitable size known initially as 'zones'. Zone commanders' appointments were approved by Army Commanders in Chief. The appointment of battalion, company and platoon commanders followed. By the end of May 1940, 400,000 men had been enrolled and the organization gradually began to take shape. At first, arm bands with the letters 'LDV' constituted the only uniform of the force until the promised denim overalls and khaki field service caps arrived, sometimes many weeks after formation. Similarly for a short period of time the only arms carried were shotguns or pitchforks.

Constitutionally the force existed under the Defence (Local Defence Volunteers) Regulations passed on 17 May 1940. On 31 July a further regulation, instigated by the Prime Minister, changed the title to 'Home Guard'. Although for the first nine months of its existence the Home Guard was recognized as part of the armed forces of the Crown, no arrangements were made for the commissioning of officers or for conferring and delegating powers of command and discipline. Consequently no appointment in the Home Guard was legally recognized as higher than private in the Regular Forces. This system of 'appointed' ranks was clearly unsatisfactory, but despite early recognition of the need for change, it was not until 12 February 1941 that the Home Guard Officers' Commission Order was passed. From that date officers and men were known by orthodox army ranks with the exception of privates who were styled 'volunteer'. This traditional title, going back many hundreds of years, was finally dropped in favour of 'private' in the spring of 1942 when Parliament took powers to order direct enrolment into the Home Guard and the force lost its exclusively volunteer character.

Relations with counties were cemented early in August 1940 when Home Guard battalions were affiliated to their local Territorial battalions and authorized to wear their cap badges. An interesting organizational difference evolved in Northern Ireland where there was not, at that time, a Territorial

Below: The German Commandant of the British Channel Isles, as he was styled in Germany, arriving at his Headquarters. A Channel Islands policeman opens his car door.

Army in existence. It was therefore decided to base the Ulster Home Guard upon the Ulster Special Constabulary. Thus the status of the Ulster Local Defence Volunteers, which did not adopt the title Home Guard until early 1942, was technically that of policemen rather than members of the Armed Forces. But all training was carried out by the army and the force, as elsewhere in the United Kingdom, was fully integrated into defence plans and would have come under military command in the event of invasion.

The overall strength of the Home Guard increased throughout the early months of its existence to reach a figure of about 1,700,000 before the end of 1940, a force three times the size originally envisaged. A peak of 1,793,000 was reached in March 1943. It remained at approximately this figure until the organization was disbanded in late 1944. The backbone of the force was the 'General Service' Battalion, the Home Guard equivalent to the infantry battalion. It was about 1,000 men strong, sometimes more, and was armed mainly with rifles and section light machine guns. As supplies became available heavier weapons such as the Northover grenade projector, the 29mm Spigot mortar and the medium machine gun were issued. These were usually grouped in heavy weapons platoons in an organization rather like an infantry battalion's support company. Signals and medical platoons tended to be part of companies, rather than battalions, a reflection of the enormous areas of responsibility often covered by Home Guard battalions.

The operational role of the Home Guard was the subject of a great deal of argument throughout its existence. In the early months, lacking as it was in both arms and training, patrolling and minor static guards were as much as could reasonably be expected from the force, which was not really at that stage integrated into overall defence plans. During 1941 the situation changed, however, as better organization, training and equipment began to make themselves felt. Home Guard battalions were included in the overall

Right: Nurses in a London maternity hospital holding babies in gas suits in the early years of the war, when the threat from gas attack was perceived as a likely one.

Below: London's tube system provided a perfect underground shelter during the Second World War. Here Londoners are shown sleeping not only on the platform of Aldwych Tube Station but also on the tracks, the electric current having been switched off. The London Underground would still constitute an effective air raid shelter system today.

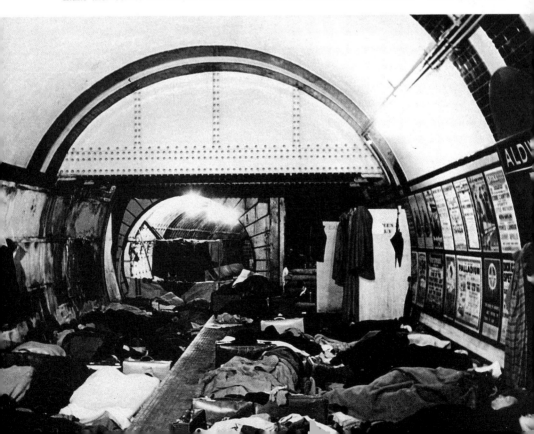

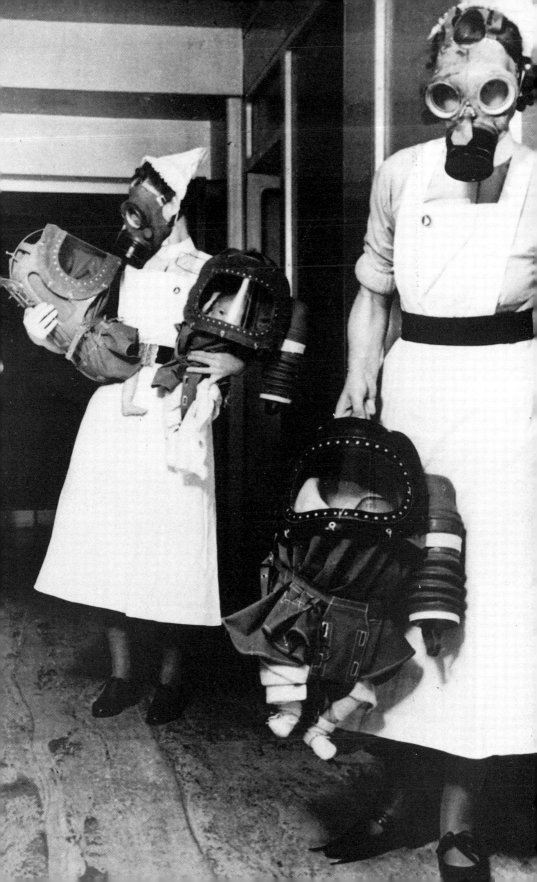

static defence scheme, which was based on 'defended localities' each incorporating one or two smaller heavily defended areas or 'keeps' as they became known. Superimposed upon this static defence system were mobile formations, exclusively Regular, which would provide containing and counter attack forces once the main thrusts of any invasion had been identified. The key role of the Home Guard was to locate and identify enemy movements, a function for which they were well suited because of their widespread coverage of the country.

The Home Guard was never allotted – and it is doubtful if it ever sought – a truly mobile role. Such a role would have depended upon armoured, artillery and comprehensive transport support, none of which was ever planned for it. Such mobility as the Home Guard ever achieved was provided largely by bicycles, with civilian cars, vans and lorries transporting or towing the heavy weapons. But this mobility was restricted to authorized mobile reserve companies intended for purely local reinforcement.

Specialized units, rather than specialist platoons within general service battalions, were generally confined to coastal defence, anti aircraft artillery and transport units. Coast defence, traditionally a role for volunteer forces since Napoleonic times, was undertaken by Home Guard companies and

Above: Home Guard practising bayonet drill on the streets of London. It is unlikely that Home Guard soldiers would have resorted to such tactics in the event of invasion, but the training was good for morale.

platoons attached to Regular coast defence installations. Some idea of how the threat to our coast was perceived in 1940 and 1941 can be gleaned from a War Office pamphlet on Coastal Defence published in April 1941. One of the paragraphs on the threat reads:

'Organisation of port and beach defences
4. It is to be anticipated that the enemy will do all he can to achieve surprise and will land on a wide front under cover of darkness and fog, natural or artificial. Use may be made of fast motor craft, probably armoured, special landing craft and amphibious tanks. Sea borne landings may be assisted by parachutists and by low flying or dive bombing air attacks. Persistent gas may be used on the flanks and choking gas at the point of landing. Flame throwers may also be employed.
These possibilities will be borne in mind when the defences are being planned.'

The possibility of invasion had been a very real one. On 16 July 1940 Hitler issued his Directive No. 16 entitled 'Preparations for a Landing Operation Against England'. The operation was given the title 'Seelowe' (Sea-lion). The plan was that the Channel would be crossed on a broad front from Ramsgate to the Isle of Wight. As a prerequisite for this the RAF had to be destroyed and the immediate sea area cleared of British cruisers. Two corridors would then be created by the laying of dense protective minefields. Long range coastal artillery would help to sanitize the area. Finally naval diversions would be staged in the North Sea and by the Italians in the Mediterranean. The aim of 'Sea-lion' would be to occupy southern England from Maldon to the Severn estuary. Some seventeen divisions were earmarked for the first wave: 90,000 men were to be put ashore on the first day, rising to 260,000 by the third day.

Like so many of the previous schemes to invade England, 'Sea lion' was abandoned for a combination of reasons: the Luftwaffe failed during the Battle of Britain to gain air superiority, the German Navy was not confident that it could establish even a local mastery of the sea, and there was a serious shortage of adequate landing craft. Finally, in 1941, Hitler turned his attention to Russia.

The first Home Guard anti-aircraft battery was raised in April 1942 and by mid 1944 a useful number of Regular anti-aircraft units had handed their responsibilities over to Home Guard batteries and troops, who manned 3.7in and 4.5in guns, rocket projectors and other light weapons. The Regular units were thereby released to join the field army assembling for the invasion of Europe. The Home Guard motor transport companies, dating from September 1942, were usually based on the nucleus of existing transport platoons in General Service Battalions. They relied entirely on civilian lorries earmarked for requisition in an emergency.

During 1943 the threat of invasion was assessed as remote and the operational role of the Home Guard, with the exception of the anti aircraft units, came under some scrutiny, even criticism. It was felt that some of its members might be better employed in agriculture and industrial production rather than in training for an event that was unlikely to happen. The War Office therefore instructed members of the Home Guard to spend as much time as possible in agriculture or war production but, at the same time, it reiterated that the threat of raids, rather than full scale invasion, remained. Indeed as the Allied landings in Europe got closer, there was even more reason to expect that the enemy would land commando or paratroops to disrupt preparations. Two steps were therefore taken to make better use of the Home Guard. First, in the autumn of 1943, some inland districts were ordered to find general service companies for a new role – that of the reinforcement of coastal areas under attack or threat of attack. Secondly, and again to counteract the decreasing numbers of Regular troops available for routine guards as the Normandy landings approached, arrangements were made for the Home Guard to undertake full time duty, both on the coast and guarding the routes to the embarkation ports.

With the Allied forces firmly ashore and fighting their way across Europe in the autumn of 1944 and with the Luftwaffe less and less able to mount even 'nuisance' raids against the United Kingdom, the grounds for keeping the Home Guard in existence had greatly diminished. 'Stand Down' was ordered from 1 November 1944 and final parades were held on Sunday 3 December. Actual disbandment did not take place until 31 December 1945.

During the five and a half years of its existence the Home Guard not only contributed much to the actual defence of the British Isles but, perhaps more important, it acted as a focus for loyal endeavour. It allowed men who were too old for regular service or who were in reserved occupations to demonstrate their desire to serve their country. In the dark days of 1940 its creation must have boosted the nation's morale. It is questionable how effective the force would have been in the event of invasion. But to judge it solely in these terms is to miss the point.

After the end of the war in Europe, the role of Home Defence was again taken over, in the main, by the Territorial Army. But in the late 1940s, when the Civil Defence organization was again being revived, some thought was also being given to the use of mobile columns of Regular and Territorial troops to assist in the event of major disasters. A paper exercise along these lines was conducted at the Army Staff College in Camberley in May 1949. The first experimental column was formed in 1953 and based at Epsom. It was composed of volunteers from the Army and the RAF, lent by the two services for a year. The rationale behind these mobile columns was that it was judged that the armed forces, as then organized and trained, would be unable to provide quickly enough adequate numbers of appropriately trained men to aid the civil power after a nuclear strike. Moreover, it had also become clear that the Civil Defence Corps had insufficient manpower to form mobile columns from its own resources. There was therefore a need for a military organization that was able to provide mobile columns of fully trained rescue personnel equipped with ambulances. So in 1954 it was agreed that the army, with some help from the RAF, would provide this second echelon for civil defence. It was to be named the Mobile Defence Corps (MDC). The army and air force were able to meet the manpower demands of a new unit because time served national servicemen were continuously available. In addition the army had extra men available following the disbandment of the Anti Aircraft Command in December 1953.

The formation of the Mobile Defence Corps was announced in the 1955 Statement on Defence. The announcement stated than an effective link between local civil defence forces and the organized bodies of the armed forces was needed and that, 'this must be a disciplined body under direct military control, consisting of service personnel and capable of rapid deployment in support of the local civil defence services wherever the need is greatest'.[2] In order to meet this need the government said it intended to establish the Mobile Defence Corps, trained and equipped for fire fighting, rescue and ambulance duties. The aim was to build up in 3–4 years a force of 48 reserve battalions each of a minimum strength of about 600 and, 'in an emergency these battalions, which will be distributed over the whole country, would be mobilized like any other unit of the reserve forces'.[3]

The Corps was formally brought into existence on 1 April 1955 with its headquarters at Pendell's Camp, Merstham, Surrey. Special training depots were set up to take 10,000 men a year for one month's full time training. On completion of this training men would be posted to serve in battalions near their homes and would be liable for 15 days' annual training per year. Unlike the TA, the MDC had no extra commitment at weekends. There were two types of battalion: a rescue battalion comprising three rescue companies giving a total of 54 rescue sections and an ambulance company with 54 ambulances, and a fire fighting battalion comprising five mobile companies, each with two fire platoons, one support platoon and six fire trucks each.

No sooner had they got themselves organized for both these roles, the Corps lost one of them. The 1956 Defence Statement, after reviewing the success to date of the MDC scheme said, 'In light of experience since the inception of the scheme and especially in view of the success of the (separate) scheme for training reservists as fire fighters ... and the difficulties of giving army and RAF officers sufficient training and practical experience in fire fighting, it has been decided not to proceed with the raising of Mobile Defence Corps battalions for fire fighting. In consequence the planned strength of the Mobile Defence Corps will be reduced from 48 battalions to 36, sustained by an annual intake of 7,000 men from the army.'[4] Thus in 1956 the MDC seems to have become manned exclusively by the army and designated for advanced rescue work only.

The MDC continued in existence in its reduced strength and function until 1959. In that year the White Paper on Defence announced that, with National Service about to come to an end, it would be necessary to disband the MDC since its reservoir of ex servicemen from which it drew its recruits would inevitably dry up. Instead the Territorial Army was to be given more specialized training in civil defence techniques. So ended a brief but interesting idea which was unique in that its functions were primarily non-combatant although its members were combatants.

It was also during the middle 1950s that the decision was taken to disband Territorial Army Coastal Artillery units. It is perhaps surprising that they lasted so long. The remains of these coastal batteries can still be seen overlooking such naval anchorages as Portsmouth, Plymouth and Falmouth. They were manned by local TA volunteers and were capable of engaging targets at twenty miles range or so out to sea. The guns were mounted within large earthworks with an underground command post and living accommodation nearby.

With the ending of National Service, the task of home defence reverted to both the Regular and Territorial Armies. This has remained the case to the present day. The threat has of course changed over the years. For many hundreds of years invasion by an enemy with the specific intention of engaging British forces in battle on British soil was a real possibility. The most consistent threat was from the French; perhaps the most widely known was from the Spanish in 1588, and the most recent was of course from the Wehrmacht in 1940. Had Goering succeeded in defeating the Royal Air Force in the Battle of Britain, Hitler would have gained the air superiority necessary to put Operation 'Sea lion' into effect. With the demise of the invasion threat, certainly from 1943, no similar threat to Great Britain has existed. The threat today is very different. But it is no less dangerous.

Notes:

1 An excellent account may be found in Frank McLynn's *Invasion from the Armada to Hitler 1588–1945*, Routledge & Kegan Paul, London, 1987.
2 1955 Statement on Defence (Command 9391, HMSO) pp. 23–4, paras. 107–13.
3 Ibid.
4 1956 Defence Statement (Command 9691, HMSO) pp. 24–5, para. 111.

2. The Threat to Britain Today

We have seen how consistently difficult it has been throughout history for our enemies to conceive, organize and implement a successful invasion of the British Isles. Nothing has changed. It would be equally difficult today. But the threat to mainland Britain in the 1990s is most unlikely to come in the form of large scale invasion. In the event of a war in Europe, the Russians would not need to occupy the British Isles in order to achieve a military victory. They would however, have to neutralize Britain.

Britain would play a crucial role in any future war in Europe. In the maritime context, the war in the eastern Atlantic, in the English Channel, in the North Sea and in the strategically vital Iceland Gap would be orchestrated from headquarters in the United Kingdom. British Trident submarines would sail from their base in Faslane, their operations directed from a headquarters in this country. The British/Dutch Amphibious Force destined for Norway would also sail from the British Isles. West coast ports would be likely to receive reinforcement convoys from North America, particularly after hostilities have started when it would probably be too risky to attempt to get into Rotterdam or Antwerp. British and US reinforcements would be fed through south and east coast ports on their way to Europe, though the Channel Tunnel (if it opens in 1993) might take some of this traffic. One way or another, it can be seen that the British Isles is by far the most important maritime base and headquarters within the NATO command. It is, after all, placed geographically almost in the epicentre of the likely area of NATO/Warsaw Pact maritime conflict.

Looked at in the context of land forces and ground installations, Britain is equally significant. The strength of the I (British) Corps in Germany more than doubles upon reinforcement by UK based troops from its peacetime strength of 55,000 to its wartime strength of 120,000. These reinforcements are a mixture of Regular and Territorial Army units and of individual reservists otherwise known as Battle Casualty Replacements. There are also a large number of logistic and communications sites on the UK mainland. Many of these are US installations – ordnance depots, satellite receiving stations, base hospitals and the like – but the majority form the entire base infrastructure for the British Army.

Perhaps the most significant aspect of the military importance of the British Isles lies in its role as NATO's 'unsinkable aircraft carrier'. There are four squadrons of US F-111 long range bombers located in bases in East Anglia and central England. Additionally there are two squadrons of RAF Tornado Interdiction bombers and two squadrons of Buccaneer long range bombers (these are in addition to the seven squadrons of RAF Strike/Attack Tornado aircraft located with RAF Germany). All these aircraft are capable of carrying nuclear weapons. Such an array of aircraft represents a major strategic threat to the Soviet Union. There are also six squadrons of US A10A Thunderbolt aircraft whose task it is to fly battlefield offensive and support missions on the Central Front. Britain is also the base for large numbers of RAF and USAF transport, reconnaissance, electronic warfare, tanker and maritime patrol aircraft.

If one adds to these military, maritime and air assets the many other war-waging installations that are situated on the UK mainland – radar sites, civilian ports and ferries, factories manufacturing defence equipment, research and development establishments, government installations and much more besides – then Great Britain must be and indeed is a target which the Russians could not afford to ignore. In fact Russian strategists have themselves made it abundantly clear how they view the strategic importance of the British Isles. One such article in an official Russian military journal[1] sees Britain's importance as stemming from several factors: it is the centre of the Commonwealth, 'the base from which British imperialism pursues its aggressive policies in many parts of the world'; it is highly industrialized, 'an arsenal of NATO, a supplier of arms to many countries'; it stands in a most favourable military – geographical position in western Europe and is the crossroads of many air and sea lines of communication; it has an infrastructure 'developed and perfected to meet the demands posed by national, NATO and US Armed Forces plans'; it contains a concentration of road and rail networks, military and civil airfields, ports, naval bases, arms and ammunition depots, nuclear stockpiles, fuel dumps and pipeline systems. The article includes maps marking ports, military storage sites and nuclear weapon stockpiles; the international communications and early warning systems based on British soil are also listed: submarine cable terminals, satellite and troposcatter stations, intelligence gathering centres, radio and radio relay

Below: This photograph illustrates the Soviet capability to project force in the shape of its bomber fleet on a global scale.

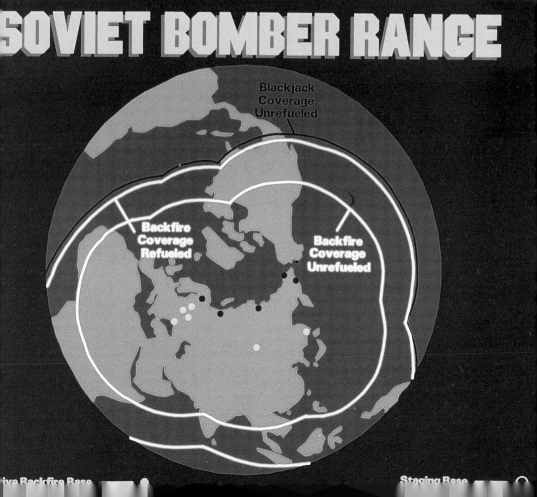

SOVIET BOMBER RANGE

Blackjack
Coverage
Unrefueled

Backfire
Coverage
Refueled

Backfire
Coverage
Unrefueled

ive Backfire Base

Staging Base

stations and the dedicated military landlines through which pass the vital communication links between the Pentagon and US Forces in Europe.

Although much of the information in this article can be collated from unclassified sources in Britain's open society, it is the detailed analysis of NATO and British installations that makes chilling reading. As we have seen, though, the Russians are so unlikely to launch a major invasion against Britain that the possibility can be discounted. Rather the threat is from sustained missile and air attack, from naval operations aimed at cutting the sea routes on which this island depends, from sabotage raids aimed at vital installations and key points and from electronic warfare and espionage in both peacetime and wartime. While the aim would most probably be to invade and occupy as much of western Europe as was military practicable at the time, it would only be necessary to isolate and emasculate Britain. How could this be achieved?

First, the Soviet Union has the capability to mount sustained and substantial conventional air attacks into UK airspace. While civilian or economic targets could be attacked it is much more likely that RAF and USAF air bases would be targeted with a view to eliminating the threat from UK based NATO aircraft to Russian operations in Europe. Although the manned bomber constitutes the main threat to the UK mainland, some Russian short range missile systems do also pose a threat. Even after the elimination of intermediate range missiles under the terms of the INF Treaty, both Scaleboard and SS-23 missiles will be able to reach the UK mainland. SS-23 has a range of 500 kilometres and, if located in East Germany, it can reach central, southern and eastern England – the area in which virtually all RAF and USAF bases are located. Scaleboard, which has a maximum range of 900 kilometres, can reach targets in the UK even if fired from the Soviet Union. There are some 60 Scaleboard launchers opposing NATO in Europe. Because of the greatly increased accuracy of these weapons they can be used without nuclear warheads.

Soviet Strategic Aviation is equipped with six types of aircraft: the Tu 95 Bear, the Backfire, the Blackjack, the M Type Bison, the Tu 16 Badger and the Tu 22 Blinder. The strike assets of the air armies include some 165 operational Bear and Bison bombers, 160 Backfire bombers, and 405 medium range Blinder and Badger bombers and more than 450 shorter range Fencer aircraft. Obviously only a proportion of these aircraft are targeted against Europe and still fewer specifically against the UK. At least half are reserved for the Asian and US theatres. But although aircraft are allocated to either the Asian, US or European theatres, the flexibility is retained to re allocate aircraft during wartime. As well as introducing new aircraft such as the Blackjack, the Russians are reconfiguring older Bear aircraft, which carry the subsonic AS-3 air-to-surface missile, to carry the newer supersonic AS-4. About forty of these reconfigured aircraft, known as Bear Gs, are operational. But it is the Backfire which would be most likely to be used against British targets. It is currently the most modern operational bomber in the Russian inventory and they are being manufactured at the rate of about thirty per year. It is thought that this production rate will be maintained till about 1990. The Backfire can undertake various missions including nuclear strike, conventional attack, anti ship strike and reconnaissance. Its low-altitude dash capability makes it a difficult aircraft to detect and engage. It has an un refuelled combat radius of 4,000 kilometres and can fly at Mach 2.

The Blackjack is a new long range bomber, larger than the US B-1B and in 1988 it was still undergoing flight testing. It is almost certain to be operational in 1989. It is thought it will have an un refuelled combat radius of about 7,300

NATO
WP

Above: A vivid illustration of the omnidirectional nature of the air threat to the UK mainland. The Soviet threat is no longer just from the east. Our air defence forces have to be capable of meeting a threat from any direction.

Right: The limited range of the Blinder bomber proved disappointing to the Soviets and they kept its production run small.

BACKFIRE

BADGER
BLINDER
BACKFIRE
FENCER

ICBM
MRBM

THE SOVIET THREAT TO UK

kilometres and a speed of about Mach 2, rather faster than the B 1B. The Blackjack will probably replace the much less capable Bison bomber and then the Bear A bomber. Its long range makes it more suitable for use against the continental USA, but it could be used against Britain.

It is not the intention to delve too deeply in this chapter into the precise capabilities of different Russian aircraft. Suffice it to say at this stage that there is a sizeable manned aircraft threat against mainland UK, targeted at the many war waging installations located in this country, but particularly against airfields launching offensive strike aircraft.

Conventional air attack on the UK would probably be backed up by a co-ordinated naval attack. The Russian Navy comprises four major fleets; the Northern Fleet, the Pacific Ocean Fleet, the Baltic Fleet and the Black Sea Fleet. It would be the Northern Fleet that would be assigned the task of breaking out through the Iceland – UK gap to cause as much havoc as they could in the Atlantic. A significant part of Russian naval strength lies in its general purpose submarine force, which consists of a fleet of some 300 submarines, the majority of which are fitted with a combination of torpedoes, anti ship cruise missiles or anti submarine missiles. The Russian submarine building programme comprises a variety of new classes of submarine, currently at least six of which are nuclear powered, and spans the whole range of undersea warfare techniques. Including older classes of submarine there are no less than ten different classes of attack submarine still deployed of which eight are nuclear powered. As with their submarines, the Soviet

Above: This artist's impression of the Blackjack bomber is probably a reasonably accurate portrayal of this new long-range Soviet bomber which is in the process of becoming operational. The Blackjack will probably replace the much less capable Bison and Bear bombers. Although its combat radius of about 7,300 kilometres makes it more suitable for use against the continental USA, it could be used against Britain.

Union's surface warships have, within the last decade, become larger and much more technologically sophisticated (examples are the *Kirov* and *Slava* class guided missile cruisers and the *Udalay* and *Sovremenny* classes of destroyers).

Two *Kiev* class VSTOL aircraft carriers are deployed in the Atlantic or North Sea and a new, larger aircraft carrier of some 65,000 tons displacement has recently been launched. But it is the submarine in particular that is the most severe maritime threat to the UK. As German U boats demonstrated during both the world wars, relatively few submarines can do great damage. The potential threat from Russian submarines today is immeasurably greater than that posed by enemy submarines in 1939. The conventional wisdom requiring an attacker to outnumber a defender on land is of course reversed in anti submarine warfare. Consequently large numbers of surface escorts, hunter killer submarines and maritime aircraft in the anti submarine role are required to protect shipping effectively. Whether NATO could deal with this sizeable threat remains in doubt. It would certainly be the Russian intention to cut the sea routes on which the British Isles depend thereby interrupting the flow of reinforcements and equipment from the US.

Despite rumours about Fifth Columnists and German parachutists during the first few years of the Second World War, there was never a significant sabotage threat to the British Isles during that period. The situation would be very different in any future war.

We know that the Russians have spent a great deal of time, energy and money developing sizeable special forces whose role it would be to operate behind enemy lines against NATO nuclear delivery means, headquarters and communication centres, airfields, key logistic installations, air defence sites, bridges and other crucial targets. When the Russians decided to develop the capability to fight and win a war in Europe if necessary without resorting to the use of nuclear weapons, they could no longer count on the nuclear strike to take out crucial targets. This necessitated the development not only of long range conventional weapons systems, but also of special forces. These special forces are known as Spetsnaz. Total Spetsnaz strength is thought to consist of 41 independent companies, 16 to 24 independent brigades, four naval brigades, twenty intelligence units, three diversionary regiments and a large number of foreign saboteurs to be activated on Spetsnaz orders. There is also some evidence to suggest that there are additional Spetsnaz units directly under the control of the GRU – the central Directorate of Intelligence of the Ministry of Defence. But the majority of Spetsnaz units work within the conventional military command structure. In each theatre of operations there is a sabotage regiment of 6–7 companies and in each Front (there are several 'Fronts' in each theatre of operations) there is one company of 'razvedchiki' (or scouts) as well as a Spetsnaz brigade consisting of 3–4 'raydoviki' (or raider) battalions and one 'vysotniki' (or special forces) company. Scouts and reconnaissance troops are also found at Army and divisional level. They are required to undertake long range reconnaissance missions, are often para-chute trained and can be considered as Spetsnaz troops. Their nearest NATO equivalent are the US Army's Long Range Reconnaissance Companies (LRRP). Raiders are retained at a higher, usually Front, level and operate in company-and-battalion sized units. They are also parachute trained and, among other roles, they are used to train partisans behind enemy lines. But it is the 'vysotniki' or special forces Spetsnaz that are the most highly trained and it is almost certainly this category that would be used in operations on the UK mainland. They are trained to operate in small teams and to accomplish deep penetration, sabotage, reconnaissance and intelligence missions behind enemy lines. They are also trained in HALO (high altitude, low opening) parachute techniques.[2]

In addition to these categories of military Spetsnaz troops there are also naval Spetsnaz. These men are the Russian equivalent of the Royal Marines' Special Boat Service (SBS). It is thought that the Russian naval infantry includes one Spetsnaz brigade which includes one VIP assassination company, one midget submarine battalion, two or three frogmen battalions and one parachute battalion. Most of the Russian naval infantry is assigned to the Baltic Fleet and would almost certainly be targeted against those parts of Denmark and Schleswig Holstein that control the exits from the Baltic into the North Sea. That is not to say that Spetsnaz could not be landed on the UK mainland by midget submarine.

The training of Spetsnaz conscripts is arduous. They are considered to be among the élite of Russian youth and priority is given to their recruitment over most other sections of the armed forces. The training of recruits includes trips to the country in whose language they are proficient and against which they would be targeted in war. These expeditions take place both openly in the guise of sporting and cultural visits and less openly when Spetsnaz operatives enter Britain as deckhands on Eastern bloc ships, cabin and flight deck crew on civil aircraft and as lorry drivers or simply as tourists. On these visits they have the opportunity to reconnoitre key strategic targets and to practise using message drops and equipment caches.[3]

Training exercises are not confined to NATO territory. One example of their scale came to the world's attention in 1981 when a Russian *Whisky* class submarine ran aground in the Stockholm archipelago well within Sweden's territorial waters. In 1982 there were further sightings of unidentified submarines in the Gulf of Bosnia and in the vicinity of Stockholm. While the exact truth will never be known for certain, we do know that NATO submarines were not involved in these incidents. One thing was certain: photographic evidence of tracks left by underwater vehicles on the seabed was produced in a Swedish investigation into the affair. It is almost certain that Russian 'mother' submarines had been disgorging mini submarines to reconnoitre the Swedish coastline, either for training purposes or in order to make contingency plans for the disruption of neutral Sweden in time of war. All this activity suggests that the Soviet Union has a well developed capability for the disruption of coastal maritime traffic and the neutralization of sea ports.[4]

Spetsnaz forces tend to specialize in one particular set of skills. The reason for this is that most are two year conscripts and it is clearly more efficient to train them thoroughly in one set of skills and to have a wide range of special forces units in consequence. While Spetsnaz troops are known to be professional and well trained, it is unlikely that they would measure up to our own SAS soldiers. Selection methods are not as harsh, they are not so exhaustively trained over such long periods and they are unlikely to have had the same degree of operational experience. It is true that they have operated with some success against the *mujahideen* in Afghanistan though they have not found this at all easy. It would be fair to say that they are more akin to our own marines or paratroops who are also trained to operate in small groups. While Spetsnaz expertise should certainly not be underestimated, the indications are that it would be possible to thwart their operations and defeat them in battle.

Spetsnaz are known to be equipped with a number of special weapons systems. In Afghanistan they have used silenced 7.62mm AKMS assault rifles although the silencer is an old design which requires the use of subsonic

Above: This sort of meeting over the North Sea – in this case between a TU-95 Bear and a Phantom FGR2 – is a regular occurrence as Soviet long range reconnaissance crews test the reaction times of the British air defence system. It is a point of honour among RAF crews that these Soviet aircraft be 'intercepted' as quickly as possible.

ammunition which reduces the effective range of the weapon to only about fifty metres. P6 silenced 9mm pistols are also known to be used. However Spetsnaz are more usually equipped with the 5.45mm AKS 74 assault rifle and the PKM 7.62mm general purpose machine gun. A group or patrol will also carry a number of RPG 7 or RPG 18 rocket launchers for stand off attack against convoys or static installations and possibly a SAM 7 shoulder fired anti aircraft missile launcher if their target is, for instance, a headquarters from which senior commanders might come and go by helicopter. In Afghanistan they have also been seen to use the BG 15 under barrel 40mm grenade launcher mounted on Kalashnikovs. They would also carry grenades, explosives for demolition purposes, a larger than usual percentage of telescopic sights and possibly AGS 17 30mm automatic grenade launchers. It is likely that they would have some form of burst transmission secure radio, probably the R 350 M man portable equipment.[5]

It is not known how many Spetsnaz are targeted against the UK. The total strength of Spetsnaz forces is probably about 30,000 men on mobilization.[6] Perhaps 1,500 of them would be English speaking specialists who would be sufficiently highly trained to be infiltrated into the UK by submarine or HALO parachute insertion techniques or who would simply arrive by scheduled air or sea passenger services during a period of tension. They could pose as tourists, sports teams, cultural groups, business men or members of diplomatic missions. Entry into UK would probably be by way of a third country. Such infiltrators would obviously wear civilian clothes and would contact sleeper agents as guides and sources of information, shelter and transport. Naval Spetsnaz would, as we have seen, infiltrate mainly by sea

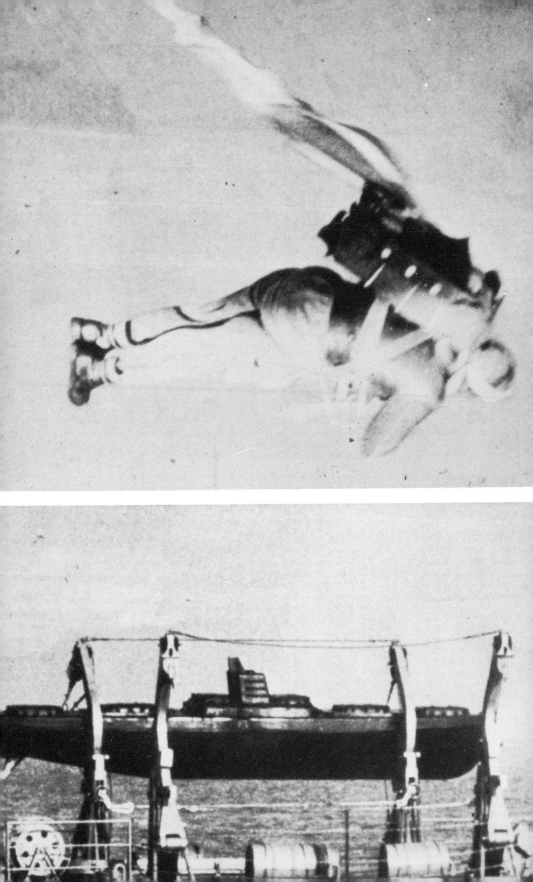

using submarines to approach close to their targets and then reach the shore in midget submarines, inflatables or by swimming. Their primary targets would be such installations as radar sites near or on the coast, the Trident submarine base at Faslane or the US naval facility at Holy Loch.

If one considers that approximately 200 IRA activists keep 10,000 British soldiers, the Ulster Defence Regiment and the Royal Ulster Constabulary relatively busy in Northern Ireland in peacetime conditions, it can be seen that 1,500 Spetsnaz would pose a significant threat in wartime.

In addition to the air and Spetsnaz threats, there would be a concentrated Electronic Warfare (EW) offensive against the UK. The NATO definition of EW is 'the deliberate radiation, re radiation, alteration, absorption, enhancement or reflection of electro magnetic energy in a manner intended to mislead hostile forces in the interpretation or use of information received by their electronic systems'. Contrary to popular belief, this is not a new threat. Electronic warfare measures were first used in anger by the Luftwaffe in the early months of the Second World War. In particular radio beams were used to guide bomber pilots to their targets over England. Later on in the war the RAF dropped thousands of tin foil strips called 'window' from aircraft to confuse German radar and locating systems. Today the Russian threat would be much more comprehensive and complex. Their aims would be to swamp or jam early warning systems, disrupt radio traffic, spoof anti aircraft systems whether ground or air launched, eavesdrop on radio conversations and electronically 'hide' the approach of their bombers.

The Russian maritime electronic eavesdropping capability is certainly the most extensive and probably the most sophisticated in the world. Specially equipped trawlers festooned with radio masts and aerials operate all over the world eavesdropping on routine radio traffic but making special efforts whenever and wherever NATO exercises are taking place. For instance during Exercise 'Brave Defender' in autumn 1985, numerous Russian trawlers suddenly appeared in the Solent to 'listen' to the progress of the Exercise. They shadow NATO warships and watch all major NATO maritime exercises.

During a period of tension and after the outbreak of hostilities this electronic assault would continue and intensify. Not only would maritime eavesdropping continue, but, more importantly, specially equipped EW aircraft would accompany bombers and fighter bombers during raids in an endeavour to jam, confuse and mislead defending aircraft. The electronic war would be keenly and cleverly fought.

It is hardly a secret that the Intelligence or espionage war has been fought with consistent intensity ever since the outbreak of the Cold War in the late 1940s. Associated with the espionage war, about which we will probably never know the complete truth, has been the Russian propaganda or disinformation offensive. Disinformation is the responsibility of Department D of the Committee on State Security or KGB. The extent of this operation only became apparent with the defection of Ladislav Bittman to the West in 1968. Prior to his defection he was Deputy Chief of the Department of Disinformation for the Czechoslovak Intelligence and security service. In his expert opinion disinformation operations by Communist countries have become more ambitious and their impact much broader in the last two decades. Alexander Yakovlev, who is Secretary for Propaganda in the Communist Party and a Politburo member since June 1987, is chief architect of Gorbachev's *glasnost* policy. In public he and his staff exude sweet reason, especially when talking to Western reporters. Yet he described the US in his book *On the Edge of an Abyss* as '. . . a country where freedom is suppressed, where violence flourishes, where trades unions are persecuted, where the

Press serves Big Business and where the basic rights of the individual are hampered: the right to work, the right to live, the right to get objective information, the right to have materially guaranteed access to true culture and the right to personal security. This is a nation in which militarism and war are the basic means of achieving foreign policy goals.'[7] Now some of this may be true but even the most critical observer of the US will agree that it is at least somewhat exaggerated. In fact it is disinformation.

Most people tend to think of disinformation as verbal or written, but it is often visual. Totalitarian states have systematically and intentionally falsified photographs for political purposes throughout the twentieth century in the Soviet Union, its client states in eastern Europe, in Mussolini's Italy, Hitler's Germany, Mao's China and Castro's Cuba. In the Soviet Union photographs have been used for disinformation since the Revolution. In the first years of its rule the CPSU, using a huge library of doctored photographs, portrayed the Bolshevik seizure of power as a mass movement headed solely by Lenin. After being purged, Trotsky 'disappeared' from many photographs including the famous one of Lenin addressing hundreds of troops in a square in Moscow in 1920.

Russian disinformation flourishes today. Topical subjects are cleverly distorted. A recent example is AIDS. Newspaper articles in the Soviet Union have alleged that the virus was manufactured in the USA. A cartoon appearing in *Izvestia* on 1 March 1987 entitled 'Death in a Flask' actually shows deadly new organisms being delivered from the 'Fort Detrick Pharmacy' to a US officer. In the background are missiles and an SDI component. This was followed by an article in *Moscow News* on 26 April which pointed the finger at Fort Detrick, Maryland as the precise spot where AIDS was created. Although admitting 'there is no direct evidence' it argues that it is 'pretty convincing' that AIDS is of US origin. But even more effective is the spreading of rumours in the Third World that AIDS is of US origin. A major goal of this campaign seems to be to create pressure for the removal of US bases overseas by suggesting that US soldiers are spreading the disease.

Much can be gleaned about Russian intentions from the invasions of Czechoslovakia and Afghanistan. The technique in 1968 was to initiate Warsaw Pact military exercises in and around Czechoslovakia early in the crisis. These troop movements were not concealed in any way – quite the reverse, they were well advertised. Thus the Russians were able to pre-position their intervention forces under the guise of exercises; they were able to make important logistic preparations and they were able to bring psychological pressure upon Dubcek who – despite his subsequent denials – must have read the possibility of invasion into the presence of thousands of Soviet troops on the borders of his country. These military manoeuvres were maintained in one form or another – there were air defence exercises, logistic exercises, exercises involving communications troops and even naval manoeuvres in the Baltic involving the Russian, East German and Polish Navies – throughout June, July and into August right up to the invasion on 22 August. Some of these exercises included some extremely clever ruses to reduce the effectiveness of the Czechoslovak armed forces. A few days before the invasion the Russian High Command succeeded in reducing the fuel and ammunition stocks of the Czechs by transferring substantial quantities to East Germany as part of a 'logistic exercise'. On top of this a further exercise was sprung on the Czech Ministry of Defence on 21 August, the day before the invasion, with the intention of distracting their attention from the build up to the invasion. In fact Dubcek ordered the army not to resist, but the Russians did not intend to take any chances.

Above: This portrayal of the Soviet Spetsnaz capability for subterfuge and deception is so over the top that it is absurd! Perhaps this very absurdity serves to make the point that this is just the sort of disguise that the Spetsnaz would NOT use. A farm or factory worker or filing clerk is much more likely.

The KGB's 'dirty tricks' department excelled themselves: in July caches of weapons, supposedly planted by imperialists, were 'discovered' on the border with West Germany; fake documents were produced to prove the existence of a 'counter revolution' actively supported by the CIA; Czech liberals were terrorised, propaganda campaigns initiated and untrue or exaggerated reports sent back to the authorities in Moscow by the KGB. In fact, the Politburo were receiving highly inaccurate information upon which to take crucial decisions. Thus the machine is capable of deceiving even itself. But all of this was subsidiary to the main deception which was to desensitise both Czech and Western leaders by the continuous series of military exercises which went on for nearly three months without a break. To what extent this was intentional will never be known. In any event it was highly successful.[8]

These examples of disinformation are relevant to out situation in the British Isles. The Russians could use these techniques to lull Western leaders into a false sense of security and to create opportunities to infiltrate agents and Spetsnaz. In a time of tension, and at the outset of hostilities Russian agents and their sympathizers would be likely to increase their activities dramatically. They would be particularly keen to gain as much Intelligence as possible on the deployment of British and US nuclear assets, particularly cruise missiles. They would wish to pinpoint UK Home Defence Command and Control, Air Defence and Early Warning assets. They would also attempt to gather the latest Intelligence on US reinforcements for Europe arriving in the UK and the progress of the deployment of British reinforcements to the continent of Europe. In particular they would wish to locate and identify as many Key Points of military significance with a view to sabotage by special forces later. Spetsnaz operating in the UK would depend for virtually all their Intelligence on files prepared by agents.

This chapter has not tried to suggest that an attack on the UK mainland is likely in the foreseeable future. The current reforms in the Soviet Union can only give us great hope for the future. Rather the aim has been to analyze the existing Russian capability for attacking the UK mainland, irrespective of current intentions. The capability is there and a *de facto* threat does exist. Thus, whatever we may assess current Russian intentions to be, we would be foolish – in the light of the history of the past forty years – to lower our guard. If we accept this premise, we must see to it that Britain possesses adequate conventional defences; the following chapters will establish whether or not it does so.

Notes:

1. Colonel V. Leskov, *Great Britain: A Strategic Survey*, Zarubezhnoe Voennoe Obvzrenie, May 1980, quoted in Michael Hickey, *The Spetsnaz Threat*.
2. David C. Isby, *Ten Million Bayonets, Inside the Armies of the Soviet Union*, Arms & Armour Press, London, 1988, pp. 88–9.
3. One such cache, containing Russian radio and cipher equipment, was accidentally dug up by a farmer in Wales in 1984. Also allegations that Spetsnaz operatives were infiltrating the CND demonstrations at RAF Greenham Common provoked controversy in 1986. See *Jane's Defence Weekly*, vol. 5, No. 3, 25 January 1986; *The Times*, 21 January 1986 and the *Sunday Times* 26 January 1986.
4. Michael Hickey, *The Spetsnaz Threat, Can Britain be defended?*, Institute for European Defence and Strategic Studies, London, 1986.
5. *Ten Million Bayonets*, pp. 90–91.
6. *Ten Million Bayonets*, p. 89 estimate is 29, 495–37,435 men. The Military Balance 1987–8, Institute of Strategic Studies, estimate is 25,000–30,000.
7. Ladislav Bittman is author of *The Deception Game* (1978) and *The KGB and Soviet Disinformation* (1986).
8. Michael Dewar, *Deception in Warfare*, David & Charles, Newton Abbot, 1989, Chap. 5.

3. Civil Protection

Civil protection is the new terminology for what has always been known as Civil Defence in Britain. While the term 'civil defence' seems to be a twentieth century notion, its origins can be traced back to the beginnings of urban history. An important part of the whole idea of a city is based upon the joint provision of physical shelter and political protection for the citizens who dwell within the city walls. It was largely by providing protection against the potential assaults of enemies that the rulers of cities gained their legitimacy. The nation state, like the city state before it, was fundamentally a security entity.

The idea that it is the duty of any civilized and legitimate government to protect its civil population receives its clearest formulation in the writings of Thomas Hobbes. In 'De Cive', Hobbes writes: 'Now all the duties of rulers are contained in this one sentence, *the safety of the people is the supreme law.*'[1] He develops this theme by stating: 'There are two things necessary for the people's defence: *to be warned and to be forearmed.*'[2] To this day, civil defence remains largely a problem of 'warning' and 'forearmament', though today this second requirement implies armament by taking shelter rather than using weapons.

Wars would appear to have increasingly involved civilians as the twentieth century has progressed. In the First World War the ratio of military to civilian casualties was 20 to 1, in the Second World War it was equal; during the Korean War it was 1 to 5, in the Vietnam War it was 1 to 20 and in any future nuclear war it could be in the region of one military death for every 100 civilian deaths.[3] Any protection for the future must be largely speculative but the trend is clear: civilians are likely to be increasingly drawn into warfare.

Civil defence is defined in international law as including various humanitarian tasks in order to enable the population to recover from the immediate effects of war, hostilities and disasters and to help its long term survival.[4] In the most simple terms civil defence is about the defence of civilians and their property as opposed to the defence of the military and military installations. And a successful civil defence assumes some sort of emergency governmental structure, probably devolved on a regional basis to cater for the possible breakdown of normal communications.

A relatively sophisticated civil defence infrastructure existed before the outbreak of war in 1939. A regional structure for the control of air raid precautions was adopted as early as 1938.[5] The selection of regional commissioners to take charge in an emergency followed soon afterwards. The UK was divided into twelve civil defence regions headed by Regional Commissioners responsible to the Minister of Home Security. GHQ Home Forces Standing Operational Instructions stated: 'In the event of an acute emergency such as that arising from a breakdown in communications, Regional Commissioners will, if necessary, exercise powers normally exercised only by Ministers of the Crown'.[6] This scheme followed very closely the pattern of the emergency organization with its 'civil commissioners' which had been worked out in the 1920s and adopted in the General Strike of 1926.

Following the successful experience of voluntary civil defence groups during the Second World War, the Civil Defence Corps was founded in 1949;

for the next eighteen years this all volunteer force epitomized the British civil defence effort. At its peak voluntary civil defence could count on more than half a million participants.[7] Then in 1968 the Civil Defence Corps was abolished largely for financial reasons and reduced to a care and maintenance basis until the 1980 Civil Defence Review. Little happened in the interim although there was a gradual evolution towards emphasis on peacetime disasters and a further commitment towards the United Kingdom Warning and Monitoring Organization (UKWMO).[8] The 1980 Civil Defence Review proposed an enhanced commitment to civil defence and a £45 million budget, a sharp increase over 1977–8 when spending was only £13.7 million. There was also a shift in emphasis so as to include peacetime disaster preparations as part of 'the essence of civil defence'.[9] In this respect British civil defence has now moved much closer to its American counterpart. As in the Second World War the population today is encouraged to stay at home. A Home Office booklet *Protect and Survive*, in a section on 'Planning for Survival' says, 'Stay at Home. Your own local authority will best be able to help you in war. If you move away – unless you have a place of your own to go to or intend to stay with relatives – the authority in your new area will not help you with accommodation or food or other essentials. If you leave, your local authority may need to take your empty house for others to use. So stay at home.'[10]

Civil Defence policy today, as enacted in the 1983 Civil Defence Regulations and later by the Civil Protection in Peacetime Act 1986, can be traced back to the successes and lessons of Second World War Air Raid Precautions. It remains today a policy which rejects emergency relocation and purpose built shelters and favours a stay put policy and self protection at home. The central government provides a warning and monitoring network and makes plans to devolve itself on to a regional basis during a crisis or in time of war. Civil defence also provides post attack or post disaster relief which is administered by trained volunteers. Only the County Emergency Headquarters which will be occupied by government officials, military commanders and welfare agency officials will be provided with a degree of protection from nuclear or conventional missile or air attack.

The alternative to this policy would be to attempt to build shelters for the whole population. This is what has been done in Switzerland. Although Swiss shelters are not capable of protecting within a mile and a half of a megaton blast and may not all be technically perfect, they have come to represent the world's standard.[11] Financially the programme has been possible because its costs were spread over a period of several decades and were shared by many different parties at national and local level. Swiss civil defence was approved by the Swiss population in a referendum, is codified in law and is built into the structure of nearly every house. It is a non partisan topic: it is part of being Swiss.

Until there is a general acceptance in the UK by the community, by local government and by all the main political parties that civil defence is for the general good, our way forward is limited to the existing, somewhat inadequate system. Even if a decision were taken tomorrow to provide communal protection for the entire nation, the sheer scale and expense of the project would probably prevent it from becoming a reality for a generation, if at all, in the complicated and cosmopolitan society of the United Kingdom.

For all its faults, what then is the system of civil defence and regional government that has evolved up to the present day? Although there have been changes in the structure of civil defence/civil protection over the years,

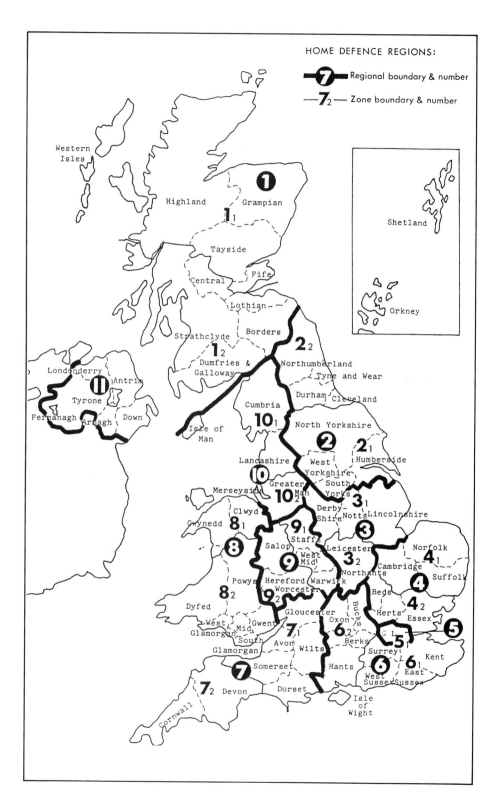

HOME DEFENCE REGIONS:

7 Regional boundary & number

7₂ Zone boundary & number

the 1948 Civil Defence Act is still the primary legislation in this field. Other legislation spells out in great detail the legal duties of local authorities to prepare plans for the care of local communities in the event of wartime disasters. Local authorities have long had the power to spend money to mitigate the effects of peacetime emergencies in their areas, but the scope of the 1948 Civil Defence Act was widened by the Civil Protection in Peacetime Act 1986 to formalize some aspects of this. All this legislation provides the legal framework for a system of Regional Government which, if necessary, would be implemented.

County Emergency Planning Officers (CEPOs) are responsible for keeping all wartime planning at county level up to date during peacetime, but in a period of international tension a Regional Emergency Committee (REC) could be formed in each Home Defence Region or County. The committees would consist of members of government departments, the police and armed services backed up where necessary by representatives of local authorities, British Telecom and the Post Office. If at any stage the ability of central government to remain in control were in doubt, regional government would be implemented. This would probably only happen in the aftermath of a nuclear attack.

There are eleven Home Defence Regions in the United Kingdom. Most Regions, except London and Northern Ireland, are subdivided into two zones. If we take No. 6 Region as an example one may understand the intricacies of regional government better. No. 6 Region is subdivided into two zones: 6.1 Zone (which includes Kent, West and East Sussex and Surrey with its zone control in Surrey) and 6.2 Zone (which includes Oxfordshire, Buckingham-shire, Berkshire, Hampshire and the Isle of Wight with its zone control in Hampshire).[12] Within each zone are a number of county war headquarters. At each of these, the County Chief Executive is the Controller (designate). Emergency powers given in a crisis will authorize his appointment in this post. From that time on he becomes an officer in the chain of regional government. If, at any time, he is isolated from Region to Zone Headquarters, he exercises the full powers of internal government within the county. The Controller would be advised and supported by the Elected Members Committee. However, in most instances the Controller would only keep the Committee briefed. He is a regional government representative and therefore is only responsible to his Zone and finally to the Regional Commissioner.

The everyday business of the county would be run by a number of groups of councillors. The Welfare Group would organize reception and housing, food control and distribution, emergency feeding and the dissemination of information to the public. The Health Group would carry out much the same duties as the environmental health services during peacetime, but problems on a much larger scale would almost certainly occur. Its main function would be the prevention of the spread of disease. Supporting the Welfare and Health Groups are the Technical and Administrative and Supply Groups. The Technical Group would be responsible for works, transport, materials and communications while the Administration Group would cover requisitioning, supply and manpower. Both groups would consist of councillors who would have the resources of council departments at their disposal and they would have the power, if necessary, to require private contractors to provide services and equipment. Working alongside the Welfare, Health, Technical and Administrative Groups would be the Control Systems Group. This is the co ordinating organization for County Wartime Headquarters. The head of this group would be advised by scientists, the police, fire service and the armed forces.

None of these bodies could function at all unless they were plugged into a system of communications. An emergency system has been developed to supplement peacetime networks. It consists of a line network rented from British Telecom and a complementary radio network engineered and maintained by the Home Office. The system links regional government headquarters to their respective county emergency headquarters and to regional HQs and to a UKWMO Group HQ. Regional government headquarters are also linked to the BBC by speech private wire circuits and to armed forces HQs by both speech and teleprinter line circuits.

Communications from county HQs down to district level also exist. In the cases of metropolitan counties and of London itself these are speech and teleprinter communications in both line and radio form. Shire counties, however, are linked to their district emergency centres by a grant aided speech only live circuit. It is planned to supplement these very limited communications by a mix of local authority radio networks and radio 'hams'. The government has agreed that specific frequencies presently used by radio hams will be set aside in wartime for radio amateurs operating on behalf of local authorities. This organization is known as the Radio Amateur Emergency Network or RAYNET. There are nearly 4,000 RAYNET members in the United Kingdom. They have an emergency call out system which can open 15–20 radio stations within twenty minutes. They regularly provide radio communications for the Red Cross and St John Ambulance Brigade. Central government grants are available to purchase radio equipment to be used by RAYNET on local authority civil defence networks. It is important that both line and radio be available to the regional government network. Although British Telecom plans to follow the safest possible routes for all its line circuits, they are vulnerable to air attack, sabotage and breakdown. Radio does provide additional flexibility.

Following widespread attacks on the country, whether conventional or nuclear, the authorities may well have to provide communal feeding and billeting facilities. Some counties are better prepared than others. One of the better prepared is Hampshire. There are more than 1,200 designated Rest and Feeding Centres within the county. Should all the premises be pressed into use they could accommodate a total of 380,000 people (or 26 per cent of the current county population). Evenly spread between the many Rest and Feeding Centres – which could be parish halls – are 29 much larger premises which have been selected at strategic points throughout the county to act as Survival Co ordination Centres. These are, in the main, large comprehensive schools. They have a large staff already on hand; they can provide shelter and emergency feeding arrangements; they are adjacent to main trunk roads. They are, in a word, able to cope with major disasters.

Local authorities would depend, to a very large extent, on voluntary organizations. The WRVS, for instance, has 165,000 members and regular helpers. They are able to set up rest centres and mass catering facilities almost anywhere. Other organizations such as RAYNET, the St John Ambulance Brigade and the Red Cross also provide voluntary help. Volunteers and representatives of the public services meet, exchange ideas and gather knowledge at the Civil Defence College at Easingwold which, since 1972, has run a series of short courses and studies bringing together people from all over the country to discuss how they would undertake their peacetime responsibilities in the extraordinary circumstances of war. They include county chief executives, senior staff and emergency planning officers from local authorities, representatives from the police, fire and ambulance services, members of the voluntary organizations and individual volunteers

in the scientific and community welfare fields. In recent years the annual throughput has risen to nearly 3,000 students.

Central government departments also plan in peacetime for war or other emergencies. The Ministry of Agriculture, Fisheries and Food is responsible for ensuring food supplies in crisis and war. Its plans would be implemented through local authorities but it is the Ministry which is responsible for maintaining food stockpiles of the basic commodities such as flour, sugar, refined fat, yeast and special biscuits – all chosen for their value as sources of energy and nutrition. These stocks are held in depots throughout the country so that they can be distributed quickly when they are needed. There is even a Ministry handbook available to local authorities on the techniques of emergency feeding and giving practical guidance on improvised cooking methods, the use of emergency equipment, methods of food preservation, etc.

The health of the nation would be a major concern in time of war and even during a major disaster. It is generally accepted that the Health Service would be hard pressed to cope with the effects of a nuclear or even widespread conventional attack on this country. In 1983 the British Medical Association published a report on the effects of a nuclear war on the United Kingdom. This concluded that much needs to be done to initiate preparations in peacetime. Central government has accordingly made money available to regional health authorities who have appointed specialist staff to produce war plans. And, more importantly, some authorities have instituted emergency stockpiles of drugs for use in wartime or a major disaster.

These and other resources need to be co ordinated. It is no good having emergency stores unless those who need to distribute them know where they are. County emergency planning officers have therefore been directed to maintain registers of resources within their own counties. A pilot study into how best this could be done was completed in Cambridgeshire, Cumbria and Northamptonshire in 1988. Examples of the types of resources which might be included are rescue equipment, building materials, transport, location of

emergency water resources, buildings capable of housing large numbers of people at short notice, and equipment which could supplement that already held by the emergency services such as lifting gear, ladders, emergency lighting and much more besides.

All these agencies – the armed services, the police and other emergency services, central government departments, local authorities, voluntary organizations – are together involved in what the government now prefers to call Civil Protection. It is an attempt to make civil defence more relevant to everyday needs. But while civil protection plans may well be implemented in peacetime in response to a major disaster, it is for war that they must be primarily intended and designed.

There can be no guarantee that the United Kingdom will never again be caught up in a war, either directly or indirectly, irrespective of what any government of the country may do in foreign or defence policy. Even if we were to drop our nuclear guard, abandon our NATO allies and submit unconditionally to any military threat, this act of faith would bring no assurance that we had freed ourselves of the possibility of some form of 'denial' attack, or that we would not suffer the consequences of a nuclear war elsewhere. Whatever policies are adopted, some element of risk would remain. Clearly Switzerland and Sweden, both neutral countries, see the logic of this argument since they have both developed highly sophisticated civil defence infrastructures. Certainly it is logical to indulge in party political polemics about the quality or type or priorities of civil defence, but it is difficult to argue that there is no need for civil defence at all.

It is instructive to look at other nations' efforts. The United States operates a nationwide civil defence system which is well staffed by both full time and voluntary workers, but, as in the UK, the populations of large cities remain vulnerable to nuclear attack. France and Germany also sustain relatively comprehensive civil defence schemes, but they too will suffer high casualties if their major cities are attacked with little or no warning.

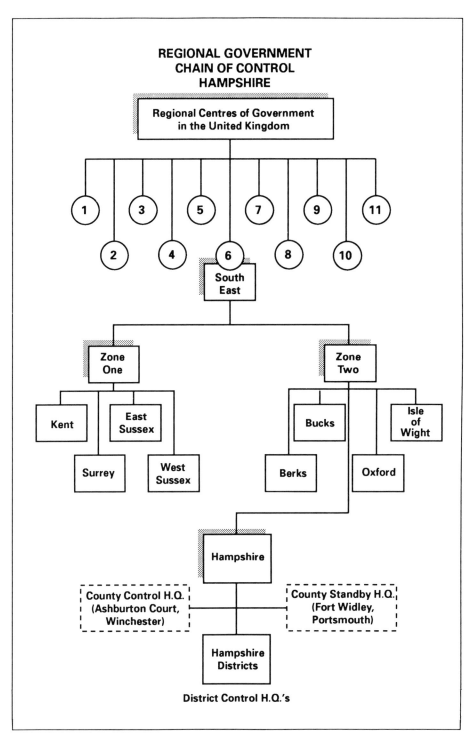

**REGIONAL GOVERNMENT
CHAIN OF CONTROL
HAMPSHIRE**

Regional Centres of Government
in the United Kingdom

1   3   5   7   9   11

2   4   6   8   10

South
East

Zone
One

Kent   East Sussex

Surrey   West Sussex

Zone
Two

Bucks   Isle of Wight

Berks   Oxford

Hampshire

County Control H.Q.
(Ashburton Court,
Winchester)

County Standby H.Q.
(Fort Widley,
Portsmouth)

Hampshire
Districts

District Control H.Q.'s

This Family Tree shows how the South East (No. 6) Region is divided into two zones and then into a number of County Headquarters. The Hampshire organisation is shown in more detail.

Perhaps the nation with the most developed civil defence system in the world is the Soviet Union. Millions of civil defence leaflets, posters and handbooks of a general and specialist nature have been distributed to the entire population. Articles on civil defence appear in specialist and popular publications; radio and TV transmit civil defence information; factories and towns hold regular civil defence exercises. Indeed civil defence training on an annual basis is compulsory, involving something like 30 million citizens and 20 million school children each year. Moreover there is some evidence that industrial plant is being relocated to the relative safety of the interior: in 1972 Defence Minister Grechko stated that '. . . the shift of production forces to the east, near sources of raw material and fuel, significantly strengthens Russian defence capability. Our factories will be less vulnerable in the event of a nuclear missile war. This will continue throughout the 1976–1980 Five Year Plan.' Although the Russians have built some shelters in their cities, they would appear to rely upon large scale evacuation for the bulk of the urban population. Perhaps only in a tightly controlled Communist society is such a comprehensive civil defence system possible.

In Denmark, a country not noted for its financial commitment to defence, legislation passed as early as 1950 lays down that private shelters must be built in all new buildings in urban areas housing two or more families or with ten or more employees. The Act also empowers the Minister of the Interior to demand shelters in existing buildings in the event of an emergency. The costs of these shelters are borne by the house owner. Public shelters, which are intended mainly for road users, are provided under Acts passed in 1949 and 1962. These are paid for by the government and their capacity is calculated to be sufficient for 25 per cent of the population.

In Switzerland, a federal decree in 1950 required the construction of air raid shelters in new buildings in communities with more than 1,000 inhabitants. This was followed in 1963 by a further Federal decree requiring localities to build public shelters where it was not possible to build private ones. Since 1978, communities with less than 1,000 inhabitants have been required to construct shelters. The present situation is that most of the population now have access to some kind of shelter or other. This programme has been funded, for the most part, by central and local government funds, though house owners have had to contribute 50 per cent of the cost of household shelters.

Sweden has been building shelters since the Second World War. At first, property owners were required to include them at their own expense in any new building. But since 1978 the government created 368 'shelter obligation localities' covering 70 per cent of the population. Within these localities shelter provision is co ordinated by local government, but if an owner is required to incorporate a shelter in his house, the extra cost – up to a predetermined limit – is borne by the state.

Denmark, Switzerland and Sweden have small populations and, in the case of the latter two, are neutral. Their situations are very different from large, heavily populated, industrialized nations such as France, West Germany and Great Britain. In one respect, comparisons with the Swedish and Swiss are not relevant. These countries are doing nothing positive to prevent war. Their entire effort is therefore directed at survival should war occur. NATO nations, on the other hand, have invested hugely in preventing war by means of deterrence. Whether or not a shelter programme in a small, heavily populated island such as Britain would be effective or financially feasible is an open question. During the war some public shelters were provided in urban areas and proved effective in reducing casualties. Morrison and Anderson shelters were provided for householders, and during the worst of the *Blitz*, the London underground system was available to the public. Also, in the first few weeks of the war 1.5 million women, children and old people were evacuated from major cities. Up until 1968 (and the disbandment of the Civil Defence Corps) plans for the limited evacuation of populations from areas close to possible military targets existed. Since that date, however, the policy of all governments has been to reject evacuation and to encourage a 'stay put' policy. Exactly the same policy exists in West Germany. In a nuclear age the United Kingdom is too small and crowded an island for an effective programme of national evacuation.

Although there is no public shelter building programme in Britain, local authorities have a statutory obligation to identify buildings which could be used as public shelters. These would be particularly necessary for people whose houses cannot provide adequate protection such as those who live in blocks of flats or for the elderly or infirm who are unable to create a protected area within their home.

There is one last major area of concern which has not been mentioned – indeed it is hardly ever mentioned, probably because it poses too difficult a question. It is the contention of the author that in the event of a NATO/Warsaw Pact conflict a purely conventional rather than nuclear attack upon the United Kingdom is not only possible but likely. What is not realized by many commentators is that a 'conventional' conflict includes chemical weapons – as far as the Russians are concerned. The Soviet Union holds a stockpile of 30,000 tons of chemical munitions and continues to add to it. NATO assumes that military targets in Britain would be attacked with chemical weapons including nerve gases. The lethal downwind hazard from such an attack could, depending on wind conditions and the type of agent used, cover an area twenty kilometres long and five kilometres wide. Service personnel are supplied with protective equipment and training, but civilians living nearby, or indeed anywhere else, are not. Clearly a programme to manufacture and stockpile respirators and protective clothing and to educate and train civilians would be controversial and expensive. No other NATO nation has grasped this nettle either. It is just 'too difficult'.

The whole civil defence arena is a minefield. It should not be, but it is. One would have thought that everybody would be in agreement about the need, if not about the details. There are many outstanding problems but the main ones are first, whether or not a comprehensive public shelter programme should be initiated. On balance, it is probably fair and logical to argue that this is just not practicable for a small island with a population in excess of fifty millions. Given time and the wholehearted enthusiasm of at least 75 per cent of the population it might be. But in the context of the democratic societies of Western industrialized nations, the consensus is unlikely to endorse more than the bare minimum of civil defence measures.

Second; if military targets in Britain are in danger of chemical attack, there is the problem of whether or not civilians should be provided with gas masks? Again the practicalities preclude an easy answer. Should one seriously consider issuing protective clothing to civilians on a wide scale? Which military bases would qualify? What would be the radius that chemical weapons would affect? The problems that would be created might be greater than those the government intended to solve: anti military sentiment, a crash in house prices in the affected areas, enormous expenditure, wholesale panic.

Third; there is the question of to what extent local authorities should be forced to implement civil defence measures by legislation. Some 10 per cent of local authorities are fully supportive of civil defence and do not need to expand their staff further at present. Some 30 per cent of authorities are acting against civil defence and will do nothing in principle until forced (these are largely the so called 'Nuclear Free Zones'). The remaining 60 per cent accept civil defence as an imposed chore. They are reluctant to be seen spending rate payers' money on civil defence, particularly if they are having to cut back on other areas. Certainly in many other European democratic nations civil defence measures have been imposed by legislation and the vast majority of the population have given their wholehearted support. Indeed in most other countries, it is a non partisan issue. Perhaps we have something to learn in this respect?

And lastly, the extent to which local authorities should contribute towards civil defence expenditure seems to be a cause of much debate. For instance, while central government provides 100 per cent grants on emergency communications equipment, emergency centres are only 75 per cent aided.

These are some of the outstanding problems in civil defence and regional government. We have a workable system. It is not perfect but it is probably about right for our particular circumstances and situation.[13] One thing is certain, it won't improve unless more people make their views felt. If ever there was a non subject in the UK, it is civil defence.

Notes:

1. Thomas Hobbes, *De Cive*, translated by Thomas Hobbes as 'The Citizen: Philosophical Rudiments concerning Government and Society' (1651), in Bernard Gert (ed.), *Man and Citizen* (Gloucester, Mass. Peter Smith, 1978), Part XIII, Section 2, p. 258.
2. Ibid, Part XIII, Section 7, p. 260.
3. These figures are those of the Swiss Federal Office of Civil Defence in their publication *Civil Defence: Figures, Facts, Data 83/84* (Berne: FOCD, 1983) p. 2.
4. These tasks include:
   a. Warning.
   b. Evacuation.
   c. Management of air raid warning precautions and blackout measures.
   d. Management of shelters.
   e. Rescue.
   f. Provision of medical services.
   g. Fire fighting.
   h. Detection and marking of danger areas.
   i. NBC decontamination and protection.
   j. Provision of emergency accommodation and supplies.
   k. Emergency assistance in the restoration and maintenance of order in distressed areas.
   l. Emergency repair of indispensable public utilities.
   m. Emergency disposal of the dead.
   n. Assistance in the preservation of objects essential for survival.
Source: Adam Roberts and Richard Guelff (eds.), *Documents on the Laws of War* (Oxford, Clarendon Press, 1982).
5. The ARP Department's first Regional Office was opened in Leeds in 1935.
6. Section 12, p. 2, para. 5.
7. Hansard, 7 February 1963, Col. 87.
8. *See* Chapter 4.
9. Home Office, *Civil Defence: Why we Need it* (London HMSO, 1981), p. 9.
10. Home Office, *Protect and Survive*, p. 7.
11. Lawrence, J. Vale, *The Limits of Civil Defence in the USA, Switzerland, Britain and the Soviet Union* (Macmillan Press, London, 1987), p. 121.
12. The author was Commander (designate) of North Hants TAOR (Tactical Area of Responsibility) in 1985–7.
13. This is the author's view. For a completely contrary view it is worth consulting Duncan Campbell's *War Plan UK, The Truth about Civil Defence in Britain*, Burnett Books, London, 1982.

4. The United Kingdom Warning and Monitoring Organization

The United Kingdom Warning and Monitoring Organization (UKWMO) is primarily an organization concerned with providing warning of nuclear attack against Britain. The main purpose of this book is to demonstrate that an attack on Britain would not necessarily be nuclear. Indeed current trends indicate it would more than likely be conventional. Thus my emphasis has inevitably been on defence against conventional attack. But the picture of the defence of Britain would be incomplete without reference to UKWMO – first because it is an organization which has received very little publicity and about which the general public knows relatively little and secondly because UKWMO, despite its primary role in the event of nuclear attack, does have a role in the conventional defence of Britain.

UKWMO's main purpose is to provide warning of conventional or nuclear attack against Great Britain. An attack having taken place, its role is to confirm and fix nuclear strikes. If this is done accurately, taking into account such factors as the type of nuclear burst (ground or air), its size (in kilotons or megatons) and the direction of the wind, other parts of the country can be warned about the likely time of arrival of nuclear fallout and the intensity of radiation that will accompany that fallout. It is fashionable to assume that little or nothing can be done to anticipate the effects of a nuclear attack. It is, of course, true that survival is unlikely if you are situated on or near Ground Zero (the point on the surface of the earth at which a nuclear device is detonated or the point on the surface of the earth above which a device is detonated in the atmosphere). However, the blast damage of a nuclear device, depending on its size, is rather less than is popularly imagined.[1] What does cause casualties is the radioactive fallout resulting from a nuclear explosion. 'Fallout' is greater the closer an explosion is to the ground since it consists of contaminated earth and debris sucked up from the surface of the earth. Explosions near the earth's surface are therefore termed 'dirty'. Lives can be saved if people can be removed from the path of this fallout in time or, if this is not possible, if they can be given sufficient warning to take certain precautionary measures which may save their lives. How is UKWMO, of which very few people have even heard, constituted?

Surprisingly the provision of an effective system of warning against air attack covering the whole country has been given a high priority by successive governments. UKWMO has been in existence for more than thirty years. It comes under the direct control of the Home Office. In peacetime it is run by a small full time staff, but during a period of international tension it can be brought up to its full wartime strength in a matter of hours – assuming that the necessary government emergency legislation has been implemented. At full strength, UKWMO is manned by thousands of volun

Right: A map illustrating the degree of coverage provided by the 25 UKWMO Group Controls sited throughout the UK. Each of the Group Controls reports to one of five sector controls: Metropolitan, Southern, Midland, Western and Caledonian. Western control is also responsible for Northern Ireland.

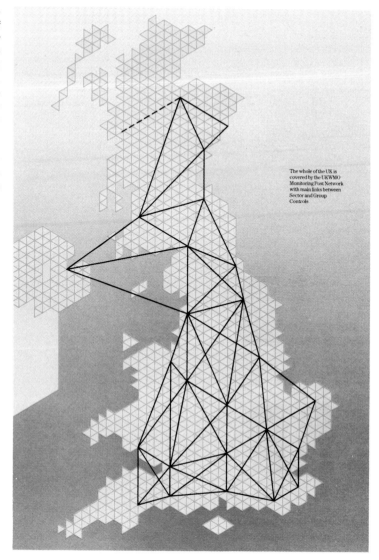

The whole of the UK is covered by the UKWMO Monitoring Post Network with main links between Sector and Group Controls

teers recruited from Home Office ranks and by members of the Royal Observer Corps (ROC) all of whom train and exercise on a regular basis in peacetime for their role in war. The Royal Observer Corps was founded during the Second World War to provide warning of the approach of German bombers. In those days they manned sandbagged observation posts in locations that were calculated to be in the likely path of enemy aircraft. Their job was not so much to provide initial warning – this was usually provided by radar – but to confirm the strength, direction and type of attack. Radar, particularly in the early days of the war, was notoriously unreliable and there were often holes in its coverage resulting from bombing attacks on coastal radar sites. With nothing more sophisticated than binoculars, an aircraft recognition manual and a telephone, the ROC provided a valuable service.

Today, information of an impending air attack on this country would come from a number of different sources.[2] These would include ground based

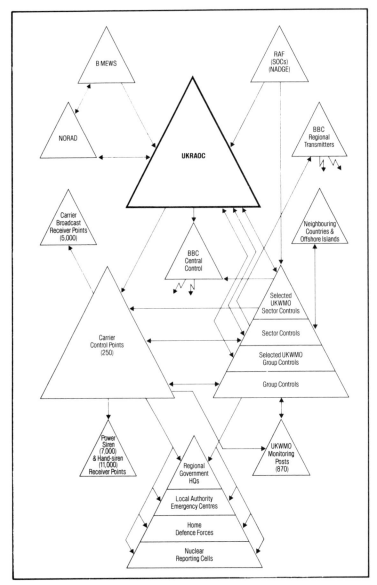

Left: UKWMD Air Attack Warning System. This diagram portrays the UKWMO air attack warning system which is in place today. An air raid warning would be initiated from the UK Regional Air Operations Centre (UKRAOC) and would be passed to the BBC, Group and Sector controls and some 250 Carrier Control Points. From these points warnings would be disseminated to UKWMO and other installations throughout the UK. It is a remarkably comprehensive system.

radars and Airborne Early Warning (AEW) aircraft to warn against attack by manned aircraft and the Ballistic Missile Early Warning System (BMEWS) station at Fylingdale on the north Yorkshire coast in conjunction with information provided by other BMEWS stations in Alaska and Greenland in the case of ballistic missile attack. All this information would be passed to the UKWMO staff manning the United Kingdom Regional Air Operations Centre (UK RAOC). They would decide, in consultation with RAF air defence experts, whether or not to set the warning network into action. The system was designed primarily to warn against nuclear attack. Turning a key at UK RAOC immediately and simultaneously alerts 250[3] locations called Carrier Control Points (CCPs) which are sited in major police stations throughout the country. In their turn the police can activate at the press of a button a total

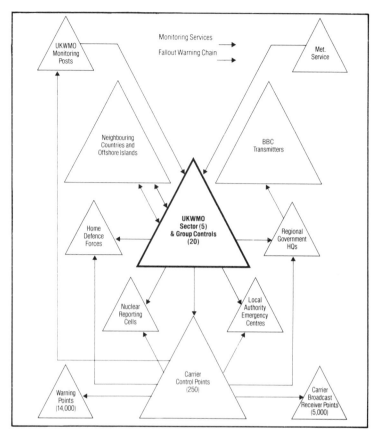

Right: UKWO Fallout Warning and Monitoring Systems. These systems follow much the same pattern as air raid warnings and make use of the same UKWO installations and communications.

of 7,000[4] powered sirens situated in major urban areas all over the United Kingdom. The CCPs are also connected to a total of a further 11,000[5] warning points in rural areas. These are located for the most part at police, fire and coastguard stations, government and service establishments, hospitals and other similar public institutions. In remote areas there are some private homes and even public houses which are, with the owner's agreement, designated warning points. CCPs and warning points are linked by means of a broadcast system which superimposes its signal on to the normal British Telecom telephone cable. The signal is amplified at the warning point by a loudspeaker. One tone informs the operator that the equipment is functioning properly and different tones provide warning of air attack, of radioactive fallout and sound the All Clear. Each warning point operator can pass on these warnings by hand siren.

Clearly all this would mean very little to the general public if they were not provided with the information necessary to interpret these signals. Sirens in peacetime normally indicate that the local fire station is having a fire practice or serve some such equally mundane purpose. Clearly there would have to be a national campaign on both radio and TV to educate the general public as to the meaning of different signals. Secondly, the staff at UK RAOC would have to be certain that the general public were threatened before they initiated such a system of general warning which was designed to meet the threat of nuclear attack. It is most unlikely that a conventional air attack on the United Kingdom would be against anything other than military targets.

Clearly it would be counter productive to cause widespread alarm if the general public were not considered at risk. It is extremely different to envisage how any UKWMO or air defence staff, however expert, would be able – initially at least – to predict enemy intentions. All one can say for certain is that the UKWMO Warning System is available and it is surprisingly comprehensive. It would reach a large proportion of the population and, assuming there had been time for a TV and radio education process, they would be able to take some precautions against air attack.

UKWMO also provides warning of nuclear fallout. There are 870 nuclear fallout monitoring posts situated throughout the UK. Each of these sends its information to one of 25 Group Controls, each of which in turn reports to one of five Sector Controls: Metropolitan, Southern, Midland, Western and Caledonian. Western control is also responsible for Northern Ireland. It is possible to exercise overall control of UKWMO from any one of the five Sector Controls. Thus, with telex, telephone and radio communications between neighbouring group controls as well as computer controlled message switching facilities, there is a degree of inter operability and redundancy built into the system so that if parts of the organization were destroyed, it could still function.

Weather information is vital for any operation of war. It affects ground operations; thick fog might dictate, for instance, that the best way of guarding a key point is by deploying a number of listening posts some hundreds of metres from the perimeter, while in good visibility an observation post within the perimeter may suffice. In good visibility quick reaction forces can travel by helicopter; in very poor visibility they may have to go by road. Air defence operations are obviously affected by weather, as are maritime operations in coastal waters. Wind conditions affect nuclear fallout patterns and are probably the main factor in determining the effectiveness of a chemical attack. UKWMO is capable of providing a comprehensive meteorological service covering the whole of Britain. Under normal circumstances UKWMO meteorological officers would merely interpret the data provided by the Central Forecasting Office at Bracknell. This would enable them to predict the pattern of radioactive fallout resulting from nuclear strikes in Europe or on the British mainland. But if for some reason Bracknell were unable to continue to provide this service, each Sector Control would be able to draw on data provided by various UKWMO meteorological assets. UKWMO is able to deploy eight radio sonds at any one time, these in addition to those monitoring posts throughout the United Kingdom (10 per cent of the total of 870) that have been equipped with sufficient meteorological instruments to allow ROC staff to provide basic data such as temperature, barometric pressure and wind direction and speed to Group and Sector Controls. Such a service is not a luxury; it is essential for updating predictions of fallout behaviour.

The 870 monitoring posts would, in times of national emergency, be manned 24 hours a day by ROC staff. In peacetime they inspect their posts, check the equipment regularly and take part in training exercises. The ROC retained their aircraft spotting role for some time after the Second World War. Now, even though it remains an independent organization, it forms an integral part of UKWMO. Typical of the chain of monitoring posts which cover the whole country is one only a few miles from a major city. It lies less than 200 yards from a main road and could easily go unnoticed. Above ground, the only signs of anything unusual are two objects, one a blue plastic dome and the other a large white canister. The first is the ionisation chamber of the fixed survey meter for measuring radiation levels and the second encases four pin hole cameras so arranged that a nuclear burst in any direction from the post would record a mark indicating the bearing and elevation of the explosion: this is the so called 'ground zero indicator'. There is also an instrument known as a 'bomb power indicator' which records the blast peak overpressure of an explosion. The ROC staff in the monitoring post would therefore be in a position to collect and collate information on nuclear strikes in their area. Their post is sunk some twenty feet below ground in a concrete chamber measuring about 7 feet × 16 feet × 7 feet in height and it is reached by means of a ladder running down a concrete shaft. The post is linked to its Group Control by telephone and to a number of Carrier Control Points. Monitoring posts have been designed to withstand the blast effects of a nuclear explosion and give protection against fallout. They have their own source of power; they have ventilation equipment, sanitation facilities and supplies of food and water. ROC staff manning them would probably be able to work and survive for a number of weeks.

The information from monitoring posts would be evaluated by the 25 Group Controls. They would be able to predict how fallout patterns are likely to develop and would issue warnings to the public as necessary. In a purely conventional conflict Group Controls would be able to act as damage control centres.

It is not particularly instructive to delve any deeper into the inner workings of UKWMO. The important fact to appreciate is that a highly developed infrastructure of trained operators, communications and data processing equipment, nuclear attack monitoring and measuring equipment and pro-tected posts exists throughout the country. It is plugged into similar organizations in the Isle of Man, the Channel Islands, Denmark, Germany, the Netherlands, France and Belgium. While the organization was designed to cope with and ameliorate the effects of nuclear attack, it would be equally useful in the event of conventional attack.

Monitoring posts are manned by a handful of ROC staff who live locally. Group Controls are manned by approximately fifty trained staff including about forty ROC members, the balance being made up by Home Office Warning Officers and scientists. Each Sector Control would need a staff of about eighty. There is absolutely nothing secret about UKWMO. Its task is purely defensive and its sole aim is to save lives. It is a product of the 1950s and 1960s when nuclear attack was considered highly likely: to the extent that this is no longer the case it can be argued that UKWMO is obsolescent. This would be a false conclusion. Nuclear attack is still possible, though unlikely. Conventional attack on the United Kingdom is also becoming increasingly unlikely, but until it becomes a virtual impossibility, it would be difficult to argue that UKWMO is not a useful resource.

Notes:

1. Some examples of blast effects are illuminating. For instance there would be no significant casualties from a one kiloton (or less) nuclear device more than two kilometres from Ground Zero. Similarly there would be no significant casualties from a 100 kiloton bomb more than ten kilometres from Ground Zero. These statistics apply to men in the open with no thermal protection. In a built up area blast effects would be reduced. For instance there would be no significant casualties from a 50 (and possibly even a 100) kiloton bomb two kilometres from Ground Zero. Men in a slit trench would survive a 200 kiloton bomb only two kilometres from Ground Zero.
2. *See also* Chapter 5.
3. UKWMO Government Information Brochure, p. 2.
4. Ibid.
5. Ibid.

5. Air Defences

The United Kingdom has been subjected to air attack twice during this century: in the First World War by the Kaiser's Zeppelins and during the Second World War by armadas of Goering's bombers. Prior to and during the Battle of Britain in the late summer and early autumn of 1940 the RAF developed a relatively sophisticated system of air defence using rudimentary radar early warning systems, Royal Observer Corps observation posts and fighter aircraft dispersed to provide the widest possible coverage. These were vectored by sector controls towards the waves of German bombers which they intercepted as best they could. We all know the story of those vital months and how they enabled Britain to hang on during the next two difficult years until the tide changed and the United States joined the war.

During the immediate post war years the air threat to the United Kingdom was ill defined. The Soviet Union was flexing its muscles and, as the Berlin Blockade showed, was prepared to indulge in dangerous brinkmanship. But in the face of the US nuclear monopoly the threat was more from attack by Russian divisions massed in eastern Europe rather than air attack against the United Kingdom. In the early 1950s, however, a major threat to Britain was posed by the first generation of post war Russian jet bombers armed at first with free fall conventional bombs and later with nuclear weapons. The squadrons of RAF Fighter Command were deployed in a large number of bases around the British coast from Leuchars in the north to Tangmere in the south, very much as they had been ten years previously during the war. Then the perception of the threat changed: The Soviet Union developed a comprehensive range of long and intermediate range surface to surface missiles armed with nuclear warheads. The logical conclusion to this increasing reliance on missiles was reached when the 1957 Defence White Paper asserted that the manned bomber was now essentially a thing of the past and that there would be no need to replace the Lightning fighter with another manned interceptor; that there was no effective defence against missile attack and that our defence posture would be based increasingly on the nuclear deterrent power of the V Bomber force. This remained the British posture throughout the 1960s and into the 1970s.

The fruits of this dangerous and short sighted policy were reaped during the 1970s: in the meantime the Russians had very wisely decided on a 'belt and braces' approach. Surface to surface missiles targeted against the United Kingdom were deployed, but at the same time new manned bombers capable of in flight refuelling and equipped with stand off weapons with both conventional and nuclear warheads were introduced. Thus by the 1970s Britain's air defence situation had deteriorated to the point where the Russians, having previously only possessed a limited offensive capability, were now capable of conducting advanced and clearly threatening long-range bombing operations against the British mainland. They were able to support this effort with an increasingly impressive air reconnaissance capability as well as the means, if necessary, to insert large or small numbers of air transported troops. In addition to all this the Russians were showing signs of closing the technological gap that had always existed between themselves and the West. This growing threat led to a complete reappraisal of the way in which Britain's air defences should be organized: clearly a comprehensive defence would be needed to meet what was an increasingly comprehensive threat.

Today the Russians possess a large strategic bomber force equipped for the most part with the Tupolev Tu-22 M 'Backfire' armed either with a bombload in excess of 12,000lb or with AS-4 'Kitchen' stand off missiles. The Russians are producing some thirty 'Backfires' a year of which half are entering service with the Maritime Air Arm and the rest with Long Range Aviation. The 'Backfire' is believed to be capable of speeds of Mach 2.2 at height and, with its subsonic range of 6,300km with in flight refuelling, it can easily attack the British mainland from any direction, while its armament of AS 4 missiles means it could, if necessary, launch its attack while still in Warsaw Pact airspace. Should it have to venture further towards our airspace it is equipped with a formidable array of ECM and ECCM equipment with which to confound interceptors.

The 'Backfire' is not the only threat. The SU-24 'Fencer' could reach Britain from its permanent bases in western Russia if it flew at high altitude for most of its route to save fuel (known as a high low high profile), or it could pose a low level threat from forward bases in East Germany. 'Fencer' carries a weapons system specialist seated beside the pilot to operate the advanced navigation and attack system which allows it to fly low level at night or in bad weather with a load significantly larger than its shorter range predecessors. Escort would be provided by later marks of the MIG-23 'Flogger' interceptor or the longer range two seat version of the MIG-25 'Foxbat'. This deadly array of aircraft is further complemented by the MIG-27 fighter-bomber armed with conventional bombs, AS-9 passive homing anti radar missiles and electro optically guided missiles and fitted with terrain avoidance radar. This comprehensive offensive capability is backed up by the An-12 and TU-16, both of which can provide stand off jamming support, while the MIG-25 'Foxbat' B and D and MiG-21 'Fishbed' H are able to undertake wide ranging photographic and radar reconnaissance.

Below: A graphic illustration of the UK Air Defence Region surface-to-air missile deployment showing the six Bloodhound sites in East Anglia and the two Rapier sites in Scotland.

The Russians now make sure that they are constantly updating and improving their capability. In 1983 the development of a new long range bomber, designated 'Blackjack' by NATO, was confirmed. Since that date the new aircraft's development programme has reached the point where its introduction into service is thought to be imminent. 'Blackjack' is larger than the USAF B-1 bomber, has variable geometry wings, is capable of long range subsonic cruise and supersonic speeds at high altitude, and low level penetration at near the speed of sound over shorter distances. It will be able to launch stand off missiles. This constantly developing air threat means that the RAF has had to develop a well organized, effective and comprehensive air defence system since the flawed Defence White Paper of 1957. Things have changed a great deal.

Bearing in mind the overwhelming advantage which surprise confers upon the attacker, our air defences have had to be structured so as to give the earliest possible warning of air attack. They must also be able to destroy enemy aircraft or missiles before they reach their target or, if this is not always possible, they must reduce the accuracy and effectiveness of this attack. In peacetime it is important that our air defence system be able to demonstrate its effectiveness and potential in war by accurately and promptly intercepting Russian reconnaissance aircraft which regularly mount missions to probe and test our defences. This requires a smooth running and efficient organizational structure.

The UK Air Defence Region (UKADR) is one of four regional command components in the integrated air defence system of NATO stretching for about 1,000 nautical miles in an arc from north of the Faeroes to the western flank of continental Europe. The UK Air Defence Ground Environment (UKADGE) system is the mechanism which actually provides warning of attack by aircraft or stand off or cruise missiles on the United Kingdom. It is linked with six other NATO Air Defence Ground Environment (NADGE) systems via the data terminal at West Drayton. Incoming data is relayed from West Drayton

Above: A Bloodhound missile at the moment of launch.

to the Air Defence Operations Centre (ADOC) at High Wycombe and from there it is dispersed to the Sector Operating Centres (SOCs) at Buchan, Bulmer and Neatishead. Each SOC is linked to a number of Command and Reporting Centres (CRCs) and Reporting Posts (RPs). Each SOC is responsible for the tactical control of operations within its designated region and the associated CRCs are responsible for tracking enemy aircraft and controlling friendly interceptors. The RPs, equipped with modern 3D radars, form the front line of detection. High capacity data links at these installations ensure that information can be exchanged securely and rapidly with other neighbouring air defence systems such as the French STRIDA air defence network, NADGE, AWACS, naval vessels, fighter aircraft bases and SAM sites. Superimposed on all this is the Ballistic Missile Early Warning System (BMEWS) at Fylingdales in Yorkshire. Its primary purpose is to provide early warning of ballistic missile attack on the continental USA, but it also provides some measure of warning of ballistic missile attack on Britain.

A formidable task faces the UKADGE system; it must be able to give the earliest possible warning of impending attack, distinguish friend from foe, quantify and prioritize attacks, communicate swiftly and clearly with all the

Right: The unrefuelled 2.5-hour CAP radius, the maximum launch range of AS-16 cruise missiles and the subsonic intercept radii from three RAF stations. The extent of the UK Air Defence Region is also shown.

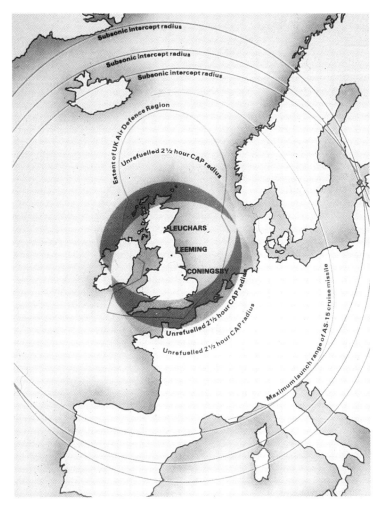

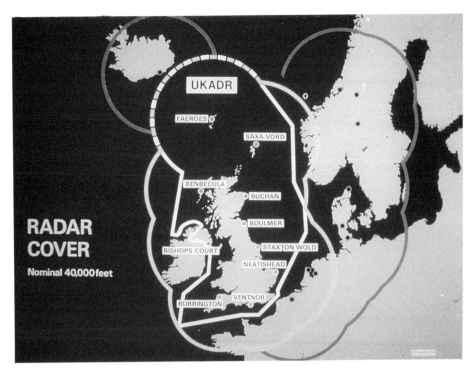

RADAR
COVER
Nominal 40,000 feet

UKADR

FAEROES
SAXA VORD
BENBECULA
BUCHAN
BOULMER
BISHOPS COURT
STAXTON WOLD
NEATISHEAD
BURRINGTON
VENTNOR

disparate elements making up the UKADGE system, concentrate and redeploy available resources, defeat enemy electronic warfare (EW) efforts and survive physical attack itself. The system is currently being modified with new radar equipment and, when complete, will provide coverage over four million square miles extending 1,000 miles from Britain's coast.

Once the UKADGE system has detected approaching aircraft or missiles, the ability to investigate and to determine identity is crucial, especially in peacetime. The ability to investigate and to discriminate belongs to the manned fighter and it is mainly for this reason that the main component part of the UK Air Defence System is made up of the RAF's fighter squadrons. These are backed up by surface to air missiles (SAMs) and some low level air defence (LLAD) guns. These must wait for the enemy to approach within range before they can engage. Fighters, however, can fly towards the enemy, they can engage the enemy farther out over the North Sea, they can switch targets more easily and, most important of all, the human brain remains more positively in control of the situation for a longer period.

The RAF has seven front line squadrons assigned to the air defence of Britain. Guarding the northern flank and the eastern Atlantic sea routes are the forces of No. 11 Group in the form of the Phantom FGIs of Nos. 43, 64 and 11 Squadrons stationed at RAF Leuchars in Scotland. Further south and guarding the approaches to East Anglia and the Home Counties are the Phantom FGR2s of No. 56 Squadron and the Phantom F4Js of No. 74 Squadron at Wattisham in Suffolk, and the Tornado F3s of Nos. 5, 29 and 65 Squadrons at Coningsby in Lincolnshire (Nos. 64 and 65 Squadrons are the wartime identities of two training formations, namely Nos. 228 and 229 Operational Conversion Units). No. 11 Squadron has just converted from Lightnings to Tornadoes and is stationed at Leeming. Thus there are now four Phantom squadrons, three Tornado squadrons and two operational conversion units,

Above: Radar cover around the UK at a nominal 40,000 ft. The inner grey range line is from UK-based radars only; the outer range line includes coverage by Iceland, Norway and non-European radars.

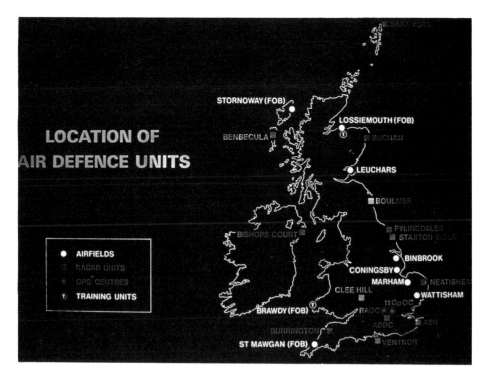

LOCATION OF AIR DEFENCE UNITS

SAXA VORD

STORNOWAY (FOB)

LOSSIEMOUTH (FOB)

BENBECULA

BUCHAN

LEUCHARS

BOULMER

FYLINGDALES
STAXTON WOLD

BISHOPS COURT

BINBROOK

CONINGSBY

MARHAM

NEATISHEA

CLEE HILL

WATTISHAM

11 Gp OC

BRAWDY (FOB)

RAOC

ASH

ADDC

BURRINGTON

VENTNOR

ST MAWGAN (FOB)

- ● AIRFIELDS
- ▦ RADAR UNITS
- ● OPS CENTRES
- Ⓣ TRAINING UNITS

Above: This map shows the loction of our Air Defence units, airfields, radar units, operations centres and training units in the UK.

making a total of seven 'front line' squadrons with two back up squadrons in wartime.[1]

The Phantom FG1s and FGR2s are two of the mainstays of several NATO air forces. They first entered RAF service in 1968. Despite the fact that both are 20 year old aircraft, they are still formidable. Their armament consists of four air to air Sidewinder heatseeking missiles and four Sparrow radar-guided longer range missiles as well as a six barrelled General Electric M-61 gun. They have a combat radius of some 500 miles with a top speed of Mach 2.1 at height and Mach 1.2 at low level where their pulse doppler radar aids detection and attack. The Phantom F4Js of No. 74 Squadron are ex US navy aircraft purchased to replace the aircraft of No. 23 Squadron now based at the RAF airfield at Mount Pleasant in the Falkland Islands.

It is, however, the Tornado F3 that is in the process of revolutionizing Britain's air defences. The RAF has ordered 165 Tornado F3s, sometimes referred to as the Tornado ADV or Air Defence Variant, which will eventually equip seven front line squadrons and an operational conversion unit, operating from three main bases at Coningsby in Lincolnshire, Leeming in Yorkshire and Leuchars in Scotland. When the Tornado re equipment programme is complete, two squadrons of Phantoms will also remain in service.

The Tornado ADV was primarily designed to counter mass raids by large numbers of relatively unwieldy bombers and strike aircraft and so more emphasis was placed on beyond visual range engagement capability than on the type of close in 'dog fighting' qualities needed in smaller scale engage-ment against highly agile fighters. The primary armament of the Tornado consists of four British Aerospace Sky Flash semi active radar homing missiles which work well with the A1-24 Foxhunter radar. The Sky Flash is a British designed derivative of the AIM-7E Sparrow, combining the airframe,

warhead and motor of the older missile with a revolutionary new seeker-head and active fuzing system. It is able to engage targets at subsonic and supersonic speeds flying at altitudes between sea level and 70,000 feet at ranges in excess of 25 nautical miles and with a 'shoot up' and 'shoot down' capability of 20,000 feet. The missile is autonomous after it has been launched and therefore gives Tornado a 'fire and forget' capability which means that multiple targets can be engaged and that the launch aircraft can manoeuvre either to attack more targets or to evade an attack itself. When Sky Flash was tested it proved to be the most successful AAM ever to be fired by the RAF, with 50 per cent of missiles hitting their targets and a further 35 per cent coming within lethal range. It really does seem that Tornado and Sky Flash are a winning combination.

For close in engagements the Tornado ADV is armed with four British Aerospace Bodenseewerk AIM-9L Sidewinders. Its advanced seeker head can detect and lock on to low intensity infra red emissions giving a real all aspect capability. Although the Tornado should normally be able to avoid getting involved in a close in turning fight, the aircraft is a perfectly capable 'dog-fighter'. Its 27mm Mauser cannon is a most effective air to air weapon, while the aircraft's swing wings and high reheat thrust (more than 16,500lb per engine!) give an impressive sustained turn rate. Another crucial advantage of the Tornado is its ability to operate with a full weapon and fuel load from 800 metres of concrete. This means that it can operate from damaged runways and that it can be dispersed well away from its home base given fuel, weapons resupply and ground crew. Smaller airfields or even suitable strips of motorway could be designated stand by airfields in wartime.

The F3 is able to operate for extended periods on combat patrols over an area stretching from the north eastern Atlantic across the North Sea to the mouth of the Baltic, down to the English Channel, and will also be expected

to contribute to the defence of the central region of Europe. In all these areas it will protect approaches to the United Kingdom and cover allied maritime forces. Without in flight refuelling the F3 can intercept a target flying 483 kilometres (300 miles) away, or 1,609 kilometres (1,000 miles) away if it is possible to transit and return at subsonic speeds. With in flight refuelling from RAF tanker aircraft the aircraft's range can be extended dramatically. Or, if range is not required, in flight refuelling can increase loiter time and allow a combat air patrol or 'CAP' to be maintained for longer periods. In this role the Foxhunter radar can track a number of targets simultaneously at a detection range of more than 100 miles. In fact tactics have been developed whereby a Tornado F3 can act as a kind of 'mini AWACS' guiding AIM-9L Sidewinder equipped Hawks on to their targets.

To ensure that this highly sophisticated weapons platform is used as efficiently as possible, the F3 is equipped with a very sophisticated weapons management, information display and communications fit enabling it to receive real time information on unidentified aircraft and jamming sources. This should allow the most economic allocation of fighter resources where they are needed most. All this makes the Tornado F Mk 3 package probably the most effective interceptor fighter in world service today.

A recent addition to the RAF's air defence capabilities are the Hawks of Nos. 63, 79, 151 and 234 Squadrons flying from Scampton in Lincolnshire,

Below: A Tornado GR 1 of 617 Squadron based at RAF Marham is seen with a Hawk of the Tactical Weapon Unit at RAF Brawdy. The Tornado is in standard NATO camouflage with underslung fuel tanks and ECM pods. The Hawk, with

Leuchars, Coningsby and Wattisham as well as their home bases of Brawdy in Dyfed and Chivenor in Devon. The Hawks, which are normally used to convert potential fast jet pilots from basic to operational flying, form an invaluable second line of defence should any enemy aircraft penetrate the outer screen of Tornadoes and Phantoms. Together with a handful of Hunters, used in peacetime to simulate enemy aircraft on exercises, the Hawks would be deployed to operate with radar equipped Tornadoes and Phantoms in mixed fighter force operations.

Using Hawk trainers to supplement Britain's air defence is an imaginative use of resources. Most jet trainers would not be up to the job, but so impressive is the Hawk's performance that it adds considerable firepower to the RAF's air defence capability. Armed with two AIM-9 missiles and a 30mm gun pod, the Hawk can patrol for one hour out to 100 nautical miles (185 kilometres) radius, or with four AIM-9 missiles out to the same range for 45 minutes' duration. Perhaps the most flexible configuration is an armament of two AIM-9 missiles, gun pod and two 190 imperial gallons (860 litres) external fuel tanks which give a duration of 2 hours and 45 minutes. It is a highly manoeuvrable little aircraft with an impressive rate of climb. Armed with the Sidewinder missile there is no doubt that it could take on most Russian bombers.

A further supplement to our fighter defences is provided by the USAF in the form of Alconbury based F-5E Tigers of the 527th Aggressor Squadron whose peacetime role is to play the part of Warsaw Pact Fighters in order to keep up the skills of NATO pilots.[2]

The time on target of all these aircraft is increased by air to air refuelling. Until 1972 all RAF interceptors were limited in range and patrol duration by their fuel capacity. But since then in flight refuelling support has been provided by Victor K2 tanker aircraft which were converted from the bomber role when the Royal Navy assumed responsibility for Britain's independent strategic nuclear deterrent. Today the RAF's in flight refuelling capability has increased and consists of the Victor K2s of 55 Squadron, the VC10 K2 and K3 aircraft of 101 Squadron and the Tristar K1 tankers of 216 Squadron. Together with other VC10s held in reserve, the RAF now has a formidable air to air refuelling capability. This maximization of aircraft usage means that interceptors can now mount Combat Air Patrols (CAP) many hundreds of miles from their bases which in turn means that hostile aircraft can be intercepted before reaching their missile release point. Using these techniques Tornadoes can now sustain a CAP between Ireland and Norway.

The aircraft is, of course, only half of the equation and it is only as good as its crew. The RAF has to ensure that its pilots and navigators are trained to an incredibly high standard, since the most modern aircraft in the most up to date air defence environment cannot hope to defeat an enemy threat unless the expertise and morale of those operating the system are of the highest order. Today's RAF is highly professional; it is staffed across the rank structure by men and women with the best technical qualifications. All pilots are graduates and only the best of this already select few are permitted to progress to jet flying. Today, the average fighter pilot will spend five weeks every year based at RAF Akrotiri in Cyprus where he will fly a number of cine camera sorties against a Canberra towing a target banner on a 250 metre line. When he has proved that he can approach this target from the correct angle he will fly at least six sorties against it firing live 30mm shells. Also the pilot will attend regular missile firing practices at ranges in remote areas of Wales and Scotland as well as practising low flying techniques in the hills.

So we have some excellent aircraft, first class pilots and navigators and the

the markings of 79 Squadron on its air defence grey camouflage, is carrying Sidewinder AIM9L missiles and a gun. Hawks such as this could provide 'top cover' for Tornado aircraft returning from an offensive mission.

Left: This photograph
shows a Victor K2
tanker aircraft of 55
Squadron refuelling a
Phantom FGR2 air-
craft somewhere over
the North Sea. Mid-
air refuelling tech-
niques ensure that
our interceptors can
mount Combat Air
Patrols many hun-
dreds of miles from
their bases. This al-
lows them to intercept
enemy aircraft before
they reach their mis-
sile release point.

Left: A Tornado F3
seen here in front of
its hardened shelter.
These aircraft shel-
ters are financed by
NATO infrastructure
funds. While not de-
signed to withstand a
direct hit, they are
capable of providing
protection from blast
damage caused by
either conventional or
nuclear explosions.
All the RAF's front line
fighters are now
housed in shelters like
this.

Left: A Tornado F3
equipped with ferry
tanks, four Skyflash
missiles and one
Sidewinder AIM-9L.

ability to keep them on station for long periods of time. The next requirement is to get this lethal package to the right place at the right time. By 1972 the low level threat from the new generation of Russian bombers and fighter-bombers was becoming apparent. Existing ground radar stations provided good medium and high level coverage, but low level cover was inadequate. To meet this threat No. 8 Squadron, based at Lossiemouth in northern Scotland, was formed. It was equipped with Shackleton AEW2 aircraft, by then redundant in the maritime reconnaissance role as they had been replaced by Nimrod. Today, the low level threat has increased, the latest technology giving the Russians the capability to attack at speeds of Mach 2 at low level from many different directions simultaneously. The Shackleton is able to provide warning of this threat far earlier than could be achieved by ground radar and can, when required, control the interceptors. Its endurance of ten hours allows it to stay on station for long periods working with interceptor crews. But the Shackleton was only ever intended to be a stop gap: the aircraft is old and its radar has a limited range and capability. The ability of Russian aircraft to launch missiles several hundred miles from our coasts made it imperative that radar coverage be extended farther out to sea by a more up to date and capable system.

The saga of the Nimrod AEW aircraft is well known and is now history. When it became clear that the British manufactured Nimrod system was not going to come up to specifications, it was decided to stage a 'fly off' between it and the by now well established Boeing E3A Sentry Airborne Warning and Control (AWAC) aircraft. The AWAC aircraft was selected and the Nimrod programme cancelled. The British AEW force will ultimately consist of eight[3] aircraft which will be stationed in peacetime at RAF Waddington, but which will deploy, in periods of tension, to forward operating bases such as RAF St Mawgan or Kinloss. The first deliveries are expected in 1991 to coincide with the completion of the UKADGE improvement programme. When combined, the interceptors, refuelling tankers, AWACS and UKADGE will together provide a fairly impressive outer layer of air defences for the United Kingdom now and into the future. Each part of the team is keenly aware of its dependence on the others and, like the Few in 1940, they are spread thinly but are highly motivated, well equipped and expertly trained.

For those enemy aircraft that might evade this outer layer of defences, a second line of defences consisting of SAMs and some LLAD guns awaits. By no means all Russian aircraft are likely to be equipped with stand off missiles. Those which are not must overfly or come very close to their targets. They will do so at high speed and at low level so as to reduce their vulnerability to fire from the ground. The RAF deploy two types of SAM: Bloodhound and Rapier. Bloodhound, although now ageing, is still a very effective system. It is a radar guided system powered by four solid propellant motors and fitted with a high explosive proximity fuzed warhead which is lethal out to a range in excess of eighty miles and at heights from 100 to 60,000 feet. There are six east coast Bloodhound sites manned by Nos. 25 and 85 Squadrons and, with an update programme to improve serviceability, the system is expected to remain viable well into the 1990s.

It is the British Aerospace Rapier system, however, which provides the most significant threat to attacking low level aircraft. It is one of the few modern systems to have been tested in actual combat conditions: during the 1982 Falklands War it is thought to have accounted for 14 of 72 confirmed Argentine kills and 6 of 14 probables destroyed by a total of 13 different weapons systems. It is a lightweight and highly manoeuverable directly-hitting missile, capable of high 'g' turns and able to maintain speeds of Mach

2 out to its maximum range of about seven kilometres. It is armed with a direct action fuze which explodes a small warhead inside the target; this, when combined with the impact force of the missile itself, ensures that even a heavily armoured target is destroyed. The fuze is immune to ECM or ground echo detonation and it has a nominal altitude capability of 10,000 feet.

Rapier comes in two distinct forms: the optical system and Blindfire which is intended to provide an all weather and night capability. The Blindfire has a single shot kill probability of 90 per cent (compared to 75 per cent for the optical system) achieved by the Blindfire radar tracker which generates a very narrow pencil beam separately tracking the target and missile and feeding error measurements to the command guidance computer. Optical Rapier's method of operation is for the surveillance radar to detect a target and automatically interrogate it with its IFF whereupon a hostile target will alarm the system and alert the operator by slewing the launcher and optical tracker to the target azimuth. The operator will then use his optics to search for the target in elevation and, having acquired it, will track it using a joystick control. Once the target is in range the computer will signal the operator to fire the missile which will automatically align to fly on to the line of sight (LOS). All the while the operator continues to track the target while a TV camera automatically tracks flares on the missile and measures any missile deviation from the LOS, feeding them to the fire unit computer where signals are generated and encoded for the command transmitter to send to the missile and maintain it on the LOS until impact. A Tactical Control Unit (TCU) makes it easier for the commander to ensure that friendly aircraft are not engaged; this is achievable because blind/priority areas can be pre set into the Rapier radar coverage which thus allows for pre arranged safe lanes at safe heights. Naturally should a hostile target appear in one of these lanes the blind arcs can be overridden and the target engaged. The TCU also has equipment which eliminates or greatly reduces the effect of enemy electronic counter measures (ECM). The success of such measures are vital to the outcome of a bombing mission since they confuse enemy defences. This electronic war of counter measures and counter counter measures (ECCM) is an area in which it is vital to keep up with and, if possible, ahead of current technology. It is also an area in which cards are played very close to the chest. Being able to spring an electronic surprise on one's opponent in air warfare confers an enormous advantage.

While Rapier provides point defence for most RAF airfields, there is one notable exception at RAF Waddington which is defended by the Skyguard system. During the Falklands War an Argentinian Skyguard anti aircraft air defence system was captured intact. No. 2729 (City of London) Squadron of the Royal Auxiliary Air Force was specially formed to man the captured system. It consists of two component parts: the first is the US manufactured Skyguard Fire Control Radar. Its radar provides early warning of a raid and allows the detachment commander to select targets for engagement. The radar together with the TV tracking system then locks on to selected targets with great accuracy in any weather by day or night. The exact target position together with details of air temperature, wind speed and direction and even the speed of individual shells as they leave the gun barrels are fed into the system computer which then calculates where each of the three guns making up a firing unit should be pointing to destroy the target.

The second component of the system is the Swiss manufactured Oerlikon twin 35mm anti aircraft gun. Each gun has two fully automatic 35mm cannon each of which can fire nine shells per second independently. Normally up to three guns with a combined rate of fire of 3,300 rounds per minute are

Above: Most RAF UK operational bases are defended by RAF Regiment squadrons equipped with Rapier surface-to-air missiles. The recent addition of Blindfire radars has given the units a near all-weather capability. This photograph shows (left) the Blindfire Radar, (centre) the Tactical Control Unit or TCU and (right) the Rapier launcher unit.

automatically laid on the target and fired under the control of the Skyguard radar, although the Commander can visually select and engage air and ground targets in his field of view. This technique was used by the Argentinians at Goose Green in April 1982 when these very same guns engaged both Harriers and attacking British paratroops with equal ferocity.

The Skyguard/Oerlikon system now deployed at RAF Waddington provides a complete air defence system for that airfield. The captured system is estimated to be worth approximately £30M and represented a not inconsiderable bonus for RAF defence spending. It is ironic that the RAF now has a highly effective gun system operationally deployed in defence of an airfield. In the late 1970s the MOD took the decision that both Army and RAF LLAD guns should be phased out altogether and that both services should rely on an exclusively missile air defence system. Virtually all other NATO armies and air forces have a mixed system recognizing the fact that neither missiles nor guns can meet every threat and that a mix of both systems is the ideal answer. Fortunately the Argentinian windfall was too good to pass by and LLAD guns are back in the British air defence armoury, albeit in a small way.

Airfields must not only be defended against attack from the air, but also from the ground.[4] This is the responsibility of the RAF Regiment which fields

Left and top left: A 2729 (City of London) Squadron Skyguard fire control radar at RAF Waddington. Together with the Swiss manufactured twin 35mm Derlikon guns (below) these two systems provide the point air defence system at RAF Waddington. The Skyguard system was captured from the Argentinians during the Falklands War and pressed into service with the RAF.

Above: This photograph shows a Tucano aircraft which is the new fixed wing basic trainer for the RAF. In war these aircraft are formed into Regional Air Squadrons providing some sort of liaison, communication and reconnaissance capability for regional military commanders.

four Light Armour Squadrons in the UK and six Royal Auxiliary Air Force Field Squadrons. These airfield defence units are organized into independent squadrons, some of them equipped with Spartan light armoured vehicles, others with the normal range of infantry weapons. Since it is not possible to secure the entire perimeter of large airfields against attacks by Spetsnaz, the RAF Regiment squadrons concentrate on guarding the key points on the base such as the hardened aircraft shelters, fuel supplies and the operations centre. At the same time mobile patrols can dominate the ground beyond the perimeter to prevent any attack against aircraft preparing to take off or land. Much has been done to prevent attack on aircraft on the ground by providing hardened shelters and blast proof walls. Camouflage, concealment and deception measures combine to mislead satellites and reconnaissance aircraft. Various measures have been adopted or are being actively investigated. These include simple methods such as the planting of trees as a screen, the use of disruption patterns on buildings or the screening of parked aircraft by large mounds. Attacking aircraft can be deceived by parking obsolescent or redundant aircraft on airfields to confuse pilots who have only seconds to discriminate between real and dummy aircraft. The RAF Regiment has been equipped with inflatable dummy Rapier systems which are designed to draw the attention and fire of attacking aircraft.

There are many aircraft in the RAF which are designed for training, liaison or communication purposes. Until quite recently these aircraft had no war role. Then it was realized that they would be able to transform the command, control and communications[5] capability of home defence forces on the ground, which were stretched in almost every respect. So they were formed into Regional Air Squadrons for Exercise 'Brave Defender' in 1985. Bulldog and Tucano basic fixed wing trainers and RAF Gazelle helicopters used for helicopter training would be able to provide a key point commander with a much more comprehensive appreciation of the scope of his task by simply flying him around his area of responsibility for ten minutes. Senior commanders can be flown from one area to another. Convoys can be escorted. There is no limit to the usefulness of these light aircraft. Should RAF resources prove inadequate there are now many privately owned light aircraft and helicopters throughout the country which would be requisitioned if necessary.

The air defence of the United Kingdom is not just about equipment. It is as much about the personnel who man the equipment. Both have to be tested at regular intervals to ensure that they are up to the mark. The most realistic test of a squadron's ability is the Tactical Evaluation or TACEVAL exercise

which takes place at regular intervals at all NATO bases. During these exercises stations are expected to operate as close to wartime conditions as is possible in peacetime. TACEVAL is a test by SACEUR of a station's ability to move swiftly from peacetime to war and of its capacity to fight. An evaluation team, which will arrive with the minimum of notice, is capable of simulating just about every situation that can affect a squadron's ability to operate efficiently. Aircraft will be declared destroyed on the ground, runways adjudged inoperable due to bombing, fuel installations destroyed, communications jammed, key commanders killed or a chemical attack initiated forcing all personnel on the airfield to wear respirators and NBC equipment. Despite all of this, the station must remain operational and interceptors have to get airborne. It is a source of some pride and satisfaction that the squadrons of

Left: A Composite Bloodhound II Fire Unit 'somewhere in East Anglia' showing (left) the small mobile type 86 radar and (right) the larger, permanently sited Type 87.

Above: This photograph shows the interior of a NATO Boeing E3A Sentry AWAC aircraft. The RAF is to be equipped with the first of these aircraft in 1991 out of a total of 8 aircraft. The RAF aircraft will form part of a NATO AWACs force.

Left: A Nimrod AEW Mk 3 aircraft in formation with a Shackleton AEW 2, an aircraft which it was due to replace before the Nimrod failed to meet specifications leading to the cancellation of the Nimrod AEW programme. Shackleton AEW aircraft will now be replaced in 1991 with Boeing E3A Sentry Airborne Warning and Control (AWAC) aircraft.

Above: The AWAC Sentry aircraft.

No. 11 Group consistently achieve a standard well above the NATO average.

As well as TACEVALS, large scale exercises with other NATO air forces take place on a regular basis. Twice yearly No. 11 Group is tested by Exercise 'Elder Joust' (until April 1987 it was called Exercise 'Priory') which is an 'in house' war game involving No. 11 Group elements only. But the main test of UKADGE integrity comes every second April when the C in C, UK Air organizes Exercise 'Elder Forest' on behalf of SACEUR. 'Enemy' aircraft provided by NATO allies include Belgian Mirage 5s and F-16s, French Mirage IVs, Jaguars and Mirage F1s, West German Alpha Jets, RF-4E Phantoms and Tornadoes, Danish Drakens and F-16s, Netherlands F-16s and USAF A-10s, F-111s and EC-130H Hercules. 'Turncoats' from the RAF include Canberras and Buccaneers operating from Norway and Tornadoes and Jaguars from RAF Germany and the United Kingdom. All these aircraft simulate enemy raids at medium and low level. Some idea of the intensity of the exercise can be appreciated by the fact that during the 1988 exercise some 150,000 low level sorties took place against Britain. For realism the exercise takes place in eastern England, Scotland and over the sea as far as Iceland. Operational heights range from sea level to 24,000 feet, but with the peacetime limit of 250 feet and 450 knots imposed over land. Incoming raids are intercepted, but for safety reasons there are no air battles. East coast missile sites get the opportunity to acquire targets and some are raided, as are fixed radar sites and underground control centres. Less easy to pinpoint are the mobile radars which increasingly are becoming the main sensors of the ground network. Groundcrew are also tested as their airfields receive fighters which have been diverted after their own station has been put out of action. These extra aircraft have to be refuelled, re armed and sheltered until needed again. Repair of battle damage to aircraft and airfields is also simulated. In war the Royal Engineers Airfield Damage Repair Squadrons can repair damaged runways in a matter of hours.[6] Thus the whole complex jigsaw of the air defence system

is exercised. About 100 aircraft are mustered to take on some 300 'aggressors' (in war some 200 air defence aircraft would be available).

This combination of rigorous training, regular practice and high quality aircraft, aircrew and ground defence personnel means that there is every chance that the United Kingdom's defence system could prevail in any second Battle of Britain.

Above: A Side Winder missile being fitted to a RAF Phantom during an exercise. It has an all-aspect attack capability and it is principally an air-to-air missile.

Notes:
1. 1988/89 Defence White Paper, pp. 76–7.
2. *See also* Chapter 9 for the role of US fighters.
3. Seven Boeing E3A Sentry aircraft have been ordered. The RAF hope to secure a total of eight aircraft to provide the necessary coverage.
4. *See also* Chapters 2 and 7 where the Spetsnaz threat against fixed installations is described in detail.
5. Command, control and communications is commonly referred to in the jargon of the armed forces as C3.
6. *See also* Chapter 7.

6. Maritime and Coastal Defence

'Britannia needs no bulwarks,
No towers along the steep;
Her march is o'er the mountain waves,
Her home is on the deep.'

(Thomas Campbell, 1777–1844)

Only a few years after this verse was written (1801) the construction of the Martello Towers – to deter an invasion by Napoleon – was started. Later, in 1860, the threat of war with France persuaded Palmerston to establish a series of massive forts in the seaward and landward approaches to Portsmouth and other naval dockyards to protect them from invasion. All of these stand today as monuments to the limitations of nineteenth century naval warfare. Coastal artillery was functioning into the 1950s and the artificial islands which served as platforms for anti aircraft defences in the Solent and off the east coast are still in position also. These defences were constructed when invasion was a possibility and large scale raids a likelihood. But, as we have already established, it is difficult to visualise circumstances in which the Soviet Union would ever wish to invade mainland Britain, certainly if her landing force were to be opposed. We are, however, with a coastline of 7,700 miles, exceedingly vulnerable to undetected infiltration by small groups of Spetsnaz bent on subversion, assassination and sabotage. These troops would probably be injected, clandestinely if possible, up to 72 hours before the Warsaw Pact commenced a full scale assault on NATO. They would have as their targets nuclear bases, command and control facilities, central government locations and personalities and other key points. Most of these troops would be landed from the sea as they would be less easily detected than if they were inserted by parachute. It would be the navy's job to detect and intercept them.

The Soviet Union has a large and growing merchant fleet. It exists to support foreign, naval and commercial policy and is controlled by central government. At a time of tension every ship in the merchant and fishing fleet would have the status of a naval auxiliary. Their potential to cause chaos in a time of tension is considerable; they will have already mapped out a detailed plan of every British port including the smallest. They will have a detailed list of any place where a few ounces of plastic explosive can do the maximum damage. In Britain virtually every port of any significance is situated on a river estuary, approached via a narrow and sometimes tortuous dredged channel. Many ports on tidal rivers have locks to maintain the water levels in their deep water berths. It has always been realized that these ports are vulnerable to mining in a conventional war. But there is little to stop a Russian merchant ship or 'trawler' scuttling herself at the narrowest part of an approach channel or entrance lock, a convenient 'accident' which could happen many days before war appears imminent.

Mining, on the other hand, would be unlikely to start until a short time before the planned outbreak of war. The discovery of mines at sea when Russian propaganda was intent on persuading the world that the West was to blame for increasing tension would not serve their cause. Rather it is likely that there would be concentrated mining at the last moment in a few key

SHETLAND

○ SUBSIDIARY HM COASTGUARD STATIONS
✛ MAJOR HM COASTGUARD STATIONS

PENTLAND

STORNOWAY

MORAY

ABERDEEN

OBAN

FORTH

CLYDE

TYNE/TEES

BELFAST

RAMSEY

LIVERPOOL

HUMBER

HOLYHEAD

YARMOUTH

MILFORD HAVEN

THAMES

SWANSEA

DOVER

HARTLAND

SHOREHAM

SOLENT

PORTLAND

BRIXHAM

FALMOUTH

areas such as the approaches to naval bases and major ports, using merchant ships, trawlers and submarines.

NATO maritime strength is, in broad terms, greater than that of the Warsaw Pact. However it is not sensible to view the maritime balance in simple ship against ship terms, not least because there are fundamental differences in the missions of the naval forces of NATO and the Warsaw Pact; NATO's concern to protect its reinforcement and resupply shipping, for example, has no parallel in the Warsaw Pact. By far the largest contribution to NATO maritime forces is made by the United States, but the availability of US ships in the eastern Atlantic at the outbreak of hostilities cannot be assumed. Thus European navies, and particularly the Royal Navy which is the largest and

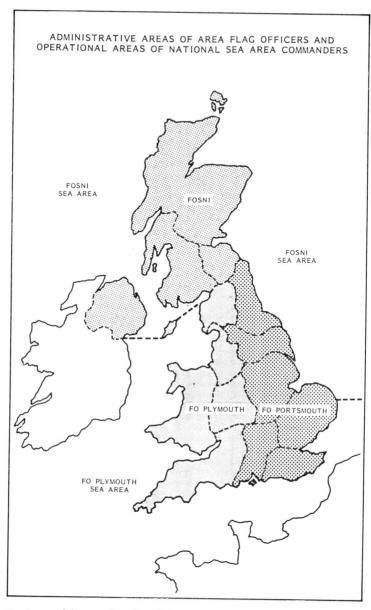

ADMINISTRATIVE AREAS OF AREA FLAG OFFICERS AND
OPERATIONAL AREAS OF NATIONAL SEA AREA COMMANDERS

FOSNI
SEA AREA

FOSNI

FOSNI
SEA AREA

FO PLYMOUTH   FO PORTSMOUTH

FO PLYMOUTH
SEA AREA

most powerful navy after that of the US in NATO, must be ready to play a
leading role in initial operations. The greatest threat of all would come from
Russian submarines, which are being added to the fleet at a rate of about one
every six weeks. This building programme compromises a variety of new
classes of submarine (currently at least six, of which five are nuclear-
powered) and all are quieter, faster, more damage resistant and able to dive
deeper than their predecessors.[1] These submarines would aim to mine
approaches to Britain and to locate and track NATO missile launching
submarines. The broad threat is a subtle one. Not since the First World War
have we faced attack by surface ships. Then German battleships shelled east
coast towns with impunity. Rather the threat now is from submarines

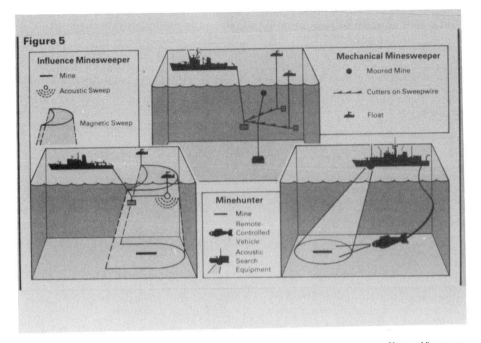

Figure 5

Influence Minesweeper
— Mine
∿ Acoustic Sweep
Magnetic Sweep

Mechanical Minesweeper
● Moored Mine
↞ Cutters on Sweepwire
⚓ Float

Minehunter
— Mine
🔵 Remote-Controlled Vehicle
🔺 Acoustic Search Equipment

attacking commercial shipping, from aircraft, merchant ships and submarines laying mines and from Spetsnaz groups landing covertly to sabotage port installations and naval bases.

Above: Minesweeping techniques explained graphically

Responsibility for the control of naval forces engaged in inshore and coastal operations in peacetime is delegated to the two Maritime Headquarters at Pitreavie and Mount Wise. These HQs are staffed to cope 24 hours a day with the normal crises which occur at sea: search and rescue, fishery accidents, pollutions and emergencies which occur on oilrigs. They would need rapid reinforcement to cope with the increased activity levels in a period of tension. Under the Maritime HQs are the Naval Officers in Charge (NOICs) in the various port HQs. The manpower for these HQs is drawn from regular naval personnel who fill peacetime shore posts as well as from the reserves and emergency lists. The NOIC, assuming he has done his homework, will have already sought the assistance of the Port Managers, HM Coastguard, the Pilotage Authority, Customs and Excise, the civil police and any other body with a knowledge of the port and its approaches. He will have to combine all their knowledge in order to manage and defend the port effectively.

The coastguards are one of the NOIC's most effective tools. Established by the Coastguard Act of 1925, the coastguard is responsible in time of war for the surveillance of our coastline. The organization is manned by about 540 regular officers, almost all of whom have seagoing experience having been recruited from the Royal Navy or merchant service. There are also about 8,500 Volunteer Auxiliary Coastguards who work in Maritime Reserve Co ordination Centres and subcentres as watchkeepers. Under the 1925 Act provision is made for coastguards to be placed under control of the Admiralty. This probably would not be necessary today; rather it has been agreed already between the Royal Navy and the Department of Transport that the coastguards would continue to contribute to coastal defence and to assist the Royal Navy in every way they can in wartime. The sort of practical help they would provide would be to establish radio communications with merchant

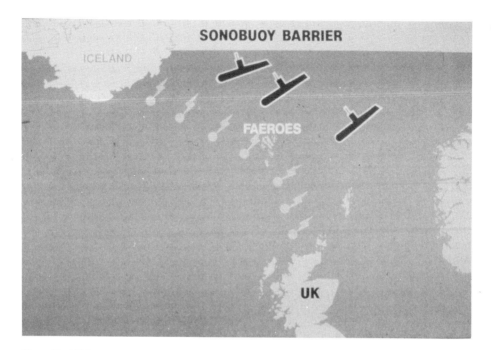

SONOBUOY BARRIER

ICELAND

FAEROES

UK

vessels, provide radar surveillance in the Straits of Dover and VHF direction finding surveillance of parts of the coastline, some boat patrols and visual surveillance of the coast from existing lookout stations.

Another invaluable organization to help NOICs is the Royal Naval Auxiliary Service or RNXS. This is a little known body of volunteers which exists specifically to support the Royal Navy in commercial ports and anchorages of defence significance during times of emergency or tension and in wartime, thereby releasing regular sailors for service elsewhere. It is a civilian, uniformed and unarmed service consisting of both male and female volunteers. They are the successors of the Royal Naval Minewatching Service (RNMWS) whose primary task was to observe the splash point of mines laid by aircraft so as to establish the limits of minefields. The RNMWS was reformed in 1952 having been disbanded at the end of the Second World War. It was reconstituted as the RNXS in 1962 and their duties included minewatching until 1976. Since that date the control of shipping and the security of ports and anchorages has become a priority, the threat of mines delivered by aircraft having receded.

At the end of 1988 the permanent staff of the RNXS numbered precisely 26 and the part time staff thirteen.[2] But the bulk of the organization is formed by approximately 3,000 volunteers who are formed into units varying in size from the smallest (of seven volunteers) in Stornoway in the Hebrides to the largest (of more than 90 volunteers) in Merseyside. Their tasks are to activate and man Port HQs, to provide ferry crews and to man patrol craft involved in the defence of ports and anchorages. A serving RN captain is appointed as Head of the RNXS. His volunteers are not paid in peacetime although they receive modest out of pocket expenses. They train for one evening a week and occasionally over weekends when two or more units might combine. Their wartime commitment and status is currently under review, but it is likely that they would serve in a rather more formal way in wartime.

Port security is in the hands of the civil, MOD and docks police. They could

UK NAVAL BASES
& SUPPLY POINTS

Faslane   Rosyth

Supply Points   Plymouth   Portland   Portsmouth

cope with most normal situations, but obviously not with a military assault. The more sensitive naval dockyards are guarded by marines or the Army, though the latter would be overstretched in meeting its priority task of guarding key points. However once the fleet had put to sea the most important assets in harbour would be merchant shipping. In most circumstances these could probably be guarded by the police and RNXS.

The protection of offshore resources, however, is very much a naval responsibility in both peace and war. The Royal Navy's Fishery Protection Squadron is responsible for looking after the nation's fishing and offshore gas and oil interests. Vessels of the *Castle, Island* and *Ton* classes are used for boarding fishing vessels of all nationalities and inspecting their papers, equipment and cargoes. Vessels that are suspected of exceeding fishing quotas are detained and escorted to the nearest convenient port for a full investigation to be carried out. The Squadron was until recently guided towards suspicious vessels by RAF Nimrod aircraft, but since this diverted precious Nimrod aircraft from their primary task of targeting Russian warships and submarines, they have been replaced by civilian aircraft under the direct control of the Fisheries Department.

The Fishery Protection Squadron is based at Rosyth in Scotland and consists of coastal and offshore divisions. The Coastal Division is made up of *Ton*-class Mine Counter Measures (MCM) vessels and patrol boats. The *Island* and *Castle* classes of patrol vessels form the Offshore Division which, in addition to its fishery protection tasks outside the 12 mile coastal limit, carries out regular surveillance and security patrols of offshore gas and oilfield installations. In addition to Royal Naval vessels and RAF Nimrod aircraft, a specially trained group of Royal Marines – known as the Comacchio Group – is available for the protection of offshore oil and gas installations. Their precise capability and *modus operandi* is classified, but it must be assumed that they would be inserted by helicopter or fast patrol craft and that they are equipped for the close defence of oil rigs. Whether or not it would be

Above: A Nimrod MR Mk 2 of 206 Squadron, RAF Kinloss, seen in the 'Hemp' camouflage, flying over an oil rig in the Moray Firth. (Photograph: Sergeant Jerry Chance, RAF PR).

possible to continue to operate all offshore oil and gas installations in wartime must be in some doubt. However they would be very difficult targets and the question of whether the Russians would wish to risk aircraft attacking this category of target is in some doubt. Moreover, if they succeeded in their aim of overunning western Europe, they would inherit the most catastrophic pollution problem in history – and that would hardly be in their interests.

The RAF contribute in a major way to the maritime defence of the nation with four Squadrons (Nos. 42, 120, 201 and 206 Squadrons) of Nimrod Maritime Reconnaissance aircraft.[3] Their role is to locate enemy surface and sub surface targets and to direct aircraft and surface ships to them. Sea Harriers operating from one of our three Anti Submarine Warfare (ASW) carriers or RAF Buccaneers armed with Sea Eagle missiles provide a long range capability to attack surface ships. But any maritime air operation would probably be co ordinated and controlled by one or more Nimrod aircraft. It is probably the most effective maritime patrol aircraft in the world. When required, two of its four Spey engines can be shut down to extend endurance and the aircraft can cruise and climb on only one engine. A wide range of weapons can be carried in the 48.5ft long bomb bay and large numbers of sonobuoys and markers can be carried and released from the pressurized rear fuselage area. In addition to its surveillance and ASW. roles, the Nimrod can be used for day and night photography. Since the Falklands conflict a hardpoint has been provided beneath each wing on which can be carried two Sidewinder air to air missiles, a Harpoon air to surface missile, a rocket, cannon pod or a mine according to the mission. It is an amazingly adaptable and flexible aircraft which, with its Searchwater radar, will be the eyes and ears of the fleet.

It is, however, the Navy's MCM and Patrol vessels that are the workhorses of the Maritime Home Defence effort. Mines would be a major threat to this country in a future conflict. During the Second World War the Germans laid 100,000 mines which sank 650 ships, while the Allies laid 250,000 which sent more than 1,000 German and Italian ships to the bottom. In the Far East the mine proved to be an even more devastating weapon, sinking more than 2 million tons of Japanese shipping. The effect of the mines was not only measured in terms of ships sunk but also in terms of men and ships diverted to countering them. By the end of the war the Allies had no less than

Below: P258 *Leeds Castle*, a Castle class patrol vessel, (top); HMS *Anglesey*, an Island class patrol vessel, (middle);and a Ton class mine-sweeper, (bottom). All these vessels operate in home waters.

Above: A Sea King Helicopter operating from the after deck of a Castle class vessel. Sea Kings can be used for anti submarine operations as well as landing marines on oil rigs.

300,000 men serving in 1,500 minesweepers while the Germans had to assign more than half their seagoing personnel to minesweeping duties. We have all seen in 1988 how effective 1939–45 vintage mines sown in the Persian Gulf have been against even the most sophisticated modern warship. The US Navy in particular were caught out badly by having no minesweeping capability available in the Gulf. The Russians would undoubtedly attempt to interfere with commercial and naval shipping, including our Polaris/Trident submarines, leaving and entering port, by sowing mines.

The old *Ton* class sweepers and hunters were, in their time, probably the best MCM vessels in NATO. They were able to deal with all types of mines and they were thoroughly rugged and reliable. In 1974 HMS *Wilton* was accepted in service. A *Ton* class vessel, she was built – unlike the first *Ton*-class ships – of Glass Reinforced Plastics or GRP. She was the first warship in the world to be built of this material. The current fleet of about twenty of this class act as either sweepers or hunters, but are being replaced by *River* class sweepers and *Hunt* class sweepers/hunters and eventually by the new Single Role Mine Hunter (SRMH), the first order for which was placed in 1985 with Vosper Thornycroft who designed and are building the vessel.

Hunt class vessels entered service in 1979. They are built of GRP and there are currently twelve in service. They are equipped with the latest minehunt ing and underwater mine disposal equipment. Every effort was made in the design of these vessels to reduce their magnetic signatures to the lowest possible level to defeat magnetic detonators. With a standard displacement of 615 tons, a length of 200 feet (60 metres) and a beam of 32 feet (10 metres), they are the largest GRP hulled ships in the world. And at £35 million each they are also the most expensive. The main reason why *Hunt* class MCM vessels are so expensive is that they are designed to deal with almost any threat. Mines can be laid with one of two objects in mind: defensive or offensive. In the defensive role they are laid in 'fields' to protect ports and convoy routes and to close off certain areas to enemy ships. In the offensive role they are laid to sink enemy ships and to prevent the use of harbours and

waterways. These offensive mines can be laid by ship, submarine or aircraft. They can even be laid clandestinely by merchant ships either immediately before the outbreak of hostilities or, with a delay mechanism, to be called into action once hostilities have started. Minehunters search for 'offensive' mines, and minesweepers clear passages through 'defensive' minefields. The *Hunt* class can do both. It has several systems to enable it to carry out its many tasks: the French–built PAP 104 unmanned, wire guided submersible, which is launched from the ship and guided along a sonar beam to its target, is the most spectacular. Its batteries are good for an hour and a half and it has enough wire to travel up to 3,000 feet (1,000 metres) from the mother ship. It carries a searchlight and a closed circuit TV camera which relays its film back to the operations room. Thus a target can be positively identified. If the decision is taken to destroy the target, the mini sub will be directed to lay an explosive charge next to the mine. Then, when the PAP 104 has been recovered to the mother ship and has been moved away to a safe distance, the charge and the target will be detonated by an ultrasonic signal.

Hunt class vessels are also equipped with the Sperry Osborn TAG acoustic system, a cylindrical generator towed behind the ship which imitates the noise not only of a ship's propeller but also of its machinery. The idea is that the quiet vessel passes safely over the mine which picks up and 'destroys' the TAG. The ship also carries the Mk II MM magnetic loop system which again is towed behind the ship and is fed with current from an auxiliary engine to set off magnetic mines at a safe distance from the non magnetic *Hunts*. Lastly, to deal with old fashioned moored contact mines, it carries an Oropesa wire sweep which has been in use for about as long as the moored mine.[4]

Then there are the *River* class fleet minesweepers which are designed to meet the threat of mines in deeper waters. This is a new class of ship of which twelve have just been completed for the Royal Navy. This sturdy 900 ton

Above: Members of the Royal Naval Auxiliary Service in the Hull Port Headquarters at work preparing a defensive patrol line.

Right: An aerial view of the after deck of a Hunt class MCM vessel. The PAP 104 underwater mine disposal submersible, which detects and neutralizes sea bed mines, can be seen in the recess in the centre of the deck. At the bottom left of the picture, again on a lower deck, can be seen the Oropesa mine sweep float to deal with moored contact mines. The mushroom shaped objects on the deck are the Sperry Osborn TAG acoustic system which consists of a cylindrical generator towed behind the ship which imitates the noise of a propeller and so detonates acoustic mines. The Hunt class MCM vessels also carry the MM Mk II magnetic loop system to detonate magnetic mines.

vessel is based on a North Sea oil rig supply ship design. Its role is that of fleet minesweeper and its task is to sweep the Russian deep water mines which would be laid off the Scottish coasts in time of war to destroy British and US submarines on their way back to their war stations. It is armed with the EDATS system with which two vessels work together towing a deep-running cable laced with explosive charges to help the mechanical cutters break the cables of moored mines. Surface vessels are relatively safe from these deep laid anti submarine mines and so the *River* class vessels, not needing a low magnetic signature, are being made of steel. As they come into service they are replacing the *Ton*-class vessels.[5]

And lastly, there is the SRMH. This vessel is designed to put the Royal Navy in the forefront of MCM vessel technology. The main requirements for the SRMH were a low noise signature, precise position and manoeuvring control at low speeds, high shock resistance, low cost and the selection of equipment that is meant to have a low development risk. All this implies a degree of compromise; for instance magnetic signature may suffer because of low cost. It will be only 160 feet (50 metres) long and 30 feet (9 metres) wide and will not be able to carry the wide variety of equipment packed into the *Hunts*. Its job will be to hunt single mines for which it will be equipped with variable depth sonar to pick up deep laid mines and also with a mine disposal system. This will probably be a dual system involving two vehicles operating from one ship, one of which will find the mine while the other will destroy it. The SMRH will have to be capable of hunting mines anywhere along the continental shelf. This will involve operating in quite deep waters. As the SMRH is a relatively small ship, the demands on the crew and the vessel itself are going to be considerable.[6]

The only category of maritime coastal defence that has not been considered in any detail is coastal artillery and shore based missiles. Although neither is currently deployed along the coasts of Britain, they remain the preferred way of protecting narrow channels in many parts of the world and, indeed, coastlines in some areas of the world. The Iranians dominated the Straits of Hormuz in the Persian Gulf during the Iran Iraq war with Chinese made Silkworm missiles and the Argentinians successfully engaged a British warship during the Falklands conflict with a land based Exocet located on the coast near Port Stanley. The Scandinavians (notably Sweden but also Norway) retain significant concentrations of emplaced artillery. The Swedes regard the defence of their harbours and base areas, strategic straits and approaches and their coastline in general as deserving the best defence that can be obtained. This means not just artillery but a balanced mix of mines, anti ship missiles, anti aircraft defences and ground forces to defend the sites themselves. The Swedes use a mix of mobile and emplaced artillery, some of it now rather elderly, but all systems are being retained until more modern equipments are procured.[7] Although the threat against Sweden is more immediate and, purely for reasons of geography and time, there is little opportunity to intercept hostile forces at some distance from the Swedish coastline (as is the case in Britain), we should monitor the Swedish use of coastal artillery. When resources are limited and priorities have to be established, it can be argued perfectly reasonably that Britain has no need of coastal defences on the Swedish model. However, in ideal circumstances some of our large naval bases might benefit from such an addition to their defences. Certainly shore based Exocet batteries located in Gibraltar would effectively deny the Straits to Warsaw Pact surface units. Another possible candidate for British deployment of coastal missiles is Port Stanley in the Falklands. Vosper Thornycroft have developed a British land based Exocet launch unit.[8]

Maritime and coastal defence of the United Kingdom is an enormously complex and challenging task. It starts with RAF Nimrods patrolling hundreds of miles from our shoreline, involves Royal Naval ships at sea hunting for and sweeping mines and fighting the anti submarine battle, and end with many different agencies, including both servicemen and civilians, undertaking the close defence of our ports and anchorages.[9] This is all co ordinated by the Commander in Chief, Naval Home Forces (CINCNAVHOME). The United Kingdom is further subdivided into administrative areas controlled by three flag officers: Flag Officer, Plymouth, Flag Officer, Portsmouth and Flag Officer, Scotland and Northern Ireland (FOSNI). The sea around our coasts is divided into only two operational areas: the FOSNI Sea Area and the Flag Officer, Plymouth Sea Area. All naval bases and ships at sea 'plug in' to this command infrastructure. It is a system which has been refined and practised in peacetime for many years. There is no reason to suppose it would not function effectively in war.

Notes:
1. Statement on Defence Estimates 1988, HMSO, London, p. 65.
2. The RNXS, RN brochure, HMSO, p. 3.
3. Statement on Defence Estimates 1988, HMSO, London, Annex C, p. 76.
4. 1987 Forces Year Book, Marshal Cavendish, London, p. 66.
5. Ibid, p. 68.
6. Ibid, p. 67.
7. Bofors Coastal Defence Artillery, *Jane's Defence Weekly*, 21 September 1985, pp. 627–31.
8. 'Coastal Defence – Some Affordable Solutions', *Armada International* 1/86, p. 72.
9. I obtained much useful detail on the defence of ports and anchorages from an article by J.F.S. entitled 'The Navy's Role in the Defence of Coasts and Harbours', in vol. 73, No. 1 of the *Naval Review* dated January 1985.

7. The Role of the Army

In the United Kingdom the Army is commanded from HQ, United Kingdom Land Forces (UKLF) located in peacetime at Wilton, near Salisbury in Wiltshire. Under this HQ are ten subordinate districts which, with one major and one minor exception, coincide with the boundaries of the Home Defence Regions:[1] The Eastern District includes two Home Defence Regions (Nos. 3 and 4) and London District has a common boundary with the London regional police boundary. Each district commander would in wartime become the regional military commander and he would be responsible to the regional commissioner and would be located with him in the regional government headquarters where he would advise on the deployment of military personnel and resources. In each region a joint service HQ would be formed, known as Armed Forces HQ (AFHQ), from which all home defence forces in the region would be directed.

Army Districts would be divided into tactical areas of responsibility (TAORs). These would normally have a common boundary with police force and county boundaries which makes liaison with both the police and local authorities a great deal easier. TAOR commanders are directly responsible to the regional military commander and AFHQ. This sort of command infrastructure requires a relatively sophisticated command, control and communications[2] system. During the early 1970s, an examination of Home Defence communications concluded that there was a need for a system which would provide communications between a mix of mobile and static units within each Home Defence Region. Accordingly, MOULD, a national Home Defence VHF/UHF network consisting of ten separate regional radio systems was conceived. It is a good example of what can be achieved using 'off the

Below: Royal Engineer Airfield Repair Regiments have all the equipment necessary to fill in craters and repair runways fit for jet aircraft to use in a matter of a few hours. Here Royal Engineers repair a damaged runway.

shelf' commercial equipment at a modest cost. The system contractor was tasked to guarantee communications between units in a number of different localities within the boundaries of each district/Home Defence Region. In the case of, for example, South West District these localities stretch from Land's End to District HQ in Bulford, near Salisbury. In the far North, HQ Scotland in Edinburgh must be able to command operations as far afield as the Western Isles, Orkney and Shetland. These sort of distances and the reliability demanded dictated a VHF or UHF system based on linked rebroadcast stations. These hilltop rebroadcast stations are an indispensible element in MOULD. There are a total of 150 of these sites. Clearly these are important locations which themselves must be designated Key Points and which must be guarded.

Under this command structure there is a sizeable military force available. There are a total of sixteen brigades based in the United Kingdom excluding 3 Commando Brigade, Royal Marines. Of these 15, 19, 24 and 49 Brigades are earmarked for the reinforcement of the British Army of the Rhine (BAOR). Another brigade sized unit called the UK Mobile Force is destined for Denmark and a further infantry battalion forms the UK contribution to the Allied Command Europe (ACE) Mobile Force. A further brigade – 5 Airborne Brigade – is always held available for operations outside the NATO area. It might or might not be available for use in Britain. But, assuming it is available, there would be a total of eleven brigades available for home defence, each consisting of three or four battalions. Some of these would be Regular battalions and some of them Territorial Army (TA). Depending on the circumstances there would be about 20 Regular infantry and perhaps 22 TA infantry battalions available for Home Defence. In addition there would be

Below: Troops from the 1st Battalion The King's Regiment deploy to defend Manchester Airport during Exercise 'Brave Defender'.

three or four armoured reconnaissance regiments equipped with Fox armoured cars, some engineers and perhaps two field artillery regiments. In a word there are precious few Regular and TA fighting units to cover the whole of the United Kingdom and the bulk of this force is infantry.

The Home Defence arrangements for Northern Ireland are slightly different mainly due to the peacetime internal security situation which has demanded a large military presence since 1969. The Ulster Defence Regiment (UDR), with more than 2,700 full time and 3,700 part time members, is organized into nine battalions consisting of 14 permanent cadre (or full time) and 36 part time companies. It is the UDR that would be primarily responsible for the Home Defence of the province though there are a few TA units as well. There is no requirement for MOULD in Northern Ireland since there is a highly sophisticated and comprehensive military communications network already in place owing to the internal security situation.

Home Defence is heavily dependent upon the Territorial Army or TA. Citizen soldiers have been defending England for hundreds of years. Indeed the oldest TA units were in existence before the Regular Army and date back to the sixteenth century. The Territorial Army is so called because it was – and is – recruited on a county or local basis; it was the successor to the Volunteer Force and was formed in 1908[3] taking a prominent part in both world wars. The TA is a national reserve designed to reinforce the Regular Army in an emergency. Ever since the ending of national service there has been a gradual erosion of the strength of the Regular Army, a reduction forced by the exponentially increasing cost of defence equipment and regular manpower. The importance and size of the TA has increased correspondingly. Today it would provide some 30 per cent of the Army's total strength in war

Below: A Cyprus Airways airliner arrives at Manchester Airport during Exercise 'Brave Defender' under the watchful eye of a GPMG Gunner of the 1st Battalion The Kings Regiment. Civil airports would be guarded from an early stage in any crisis.

and more than 50 per cent of the Home Defence forces. At full strength the TA comprises some 75,000 volunteers; and it is an impressively cost effective organization; comprising 30 per cent of total military manpower, it consumes only about 5 per cent of the Army budget.

There are three main categories of TA units: Independent units, Sponsored units and the Home Service Force or HSF. Independent units make up the largest single category of the TA. They are recruited locally and have their own regular permanent staff and their own premises called TA Centres where they keep most of their equipment. They require their members to attend a two week annual camp and a minimum of twelve days' training which usually takes place over weekends. Sponsored units are mainly technical and specialist units which recruit countrywide. They do not have their own premises, permanent staff or equipment. Instead they are sponsored by a Regular Army establishment of their parent Arm or Service; in other words, if they are specialist engineer divers they will be sponsored by a Royal Engineer establishment. These sponsoring headquarters are responsible for mobilizing these volunteers in an emergency. Like the independent units, they also have a training obligation of a two week camp annually but only four days or two weekends additional training. TA volunteers, whether joining independent or sponsored units, enlist for an initial period of three years and can prolong their service if they wish for further periods of two, three or four years. Pay approximates to Regular Army rates for every complete day's training. Many volunteers, particularly the self employed or unemployed, find themselves volunteering for much more than the minimum requirement of training days. If, however, volunteers find that they cannot meet their commitment to the TA, it is not difficult to resign. Age limits vary from 17 to 46 according to the type of units and also depending on previous military experience.

Above: Soldiers of the 1st Battalion The King's Regiment deployed to defend Liverpool docks on 'Brave Defender'. Their main task would be to prevent sabotage of dock installations.

The most recently formed part of the TA is the Home Service Force which received considerable publicity when the idea was first made public in 1980. Inevitably it attracted such epithets as 'Dad's Army', but in fact it bears little or no resemblance to the Home Guard of the Second World War. It began as a pilot scheme of only four companies in 1982 and, because of the initial success of the scheme, the decision was taken to expand the force to a total of 47 companies (or 4,500 men) by 1990. Each company is to consist of three rifle platoons and a company HQ. The platoons are attached to existing TA infantry companies and benefit from all their facilities. The task of the HSF is to defend vital installations throughout the country thus releasing Regular Army units for other tasks. The minimum age for enlistment is 20 with the exception of volunteers from the Regular Army Reserve of Officers (RARO) who may enlist from the age of 40. The maximum age for enlistment for all ranks is 50 though exceptions may be made for RARO volunteers up to the age of 55. The maximum retention age for all ranks is 60. However, some military experience is a prerequisite for joining the HSF, either in the Regular Army, TA or Army Cadet Force as an Adult Instructor. Like the TA, members of the HSF can be called up 'when national danger is imminent or a great emergency has arisen' or 'when warlike operations are in preparation or progress' or 'in defence against actual or apprehended attack'.[4] However, unlike the TA, they will not be required to serve outside the United Kingdom, the Channel Islands or the Isle of Man.

The HSF is in its infancy, but recruiting is going well and there is little doubt that the recruiting target of 4,500 men will be met. There are many ex-soldiers who are keen to undertake some form of military service, but do not have sufficient time to join an independent or sponsored TA unit. Volunteers in the HSF are only required to attend six obligatory days of training and are expected to attend a further four voluntary days throughout the year. The training requirement is: proficiency in the handling of a self loading rifle (SLR) and the ability to guard a Key Point. In this respect the HSF is similar to the old Home Guard, but it is undoubtedly more professional and better trained.[5]

As well as Regular soldiers, the TA and the HSF there are two further sources of military manpower for Home Defence. First, at any one time in the Army there are several thousand trainees in the pipeline. Training establishments throughout the country are training Adult Recruits for a period of 19 weeks, Junior Soldiers for a period of 6 months and Junior Leaders or Apprentices for a period of nearly a year. In the case of Adult Recruits who have nearly completed their training, they are likely in an emergency to be posted to their battalions a few weeks early. However, the bulk of Adult Recruits and probably all Junior Soldiers and Junior Leaders and Apprentices, who would be too young and insufficiently trained to be posted to battalions, would be retained by training depots and formed into so called Composite General Reserves or CGRs. These are company sized units that would be sufficiently well trained for most Home Defence tasks. They would be armed with normal infantry small arms, equipped with radios and transported either in military trucks or hired civilian transport. Dormant Hire schemes whereby vans become available for Home Defence exercises or in time of actual national emergency are already in existence.

Secondly, organizations known as General Support Units or GSUs, consisting entirely of reservists, report to certain Regular Army establishments where they receive a degree of refresher training, depending on the time available, and then form into company sized units. All ex Regular soldiers are committed to varying lengths of time in the Reserve depending on how long they served as Regulars. Thus there is always a pool of many thousands of experienced men, some of whom are deployed to Germany but many of whom form GSUs for Home Defence. All Reservists report on an annual basis for one day's training when they have their equipment checked, are documented and paid their annual bounty, and complete some basic training including firing a rifle. This is the absolute bare minimum to keep them in touch with developments since they left the Regular Army, but is probably sufficient to enable them to guard a static Key Point.

The SA80 rifle and Light Support Weapon or LSW are the standard weapons of the Regular Army and TA units, though it will be some years before the TA is completely equipped with them. A decision has yet to be taken as to whether the HSF will be armed with the SA80 or retain the SLR. Reservists are likely to be armed with the SLR in the immediate future, although the longer the SA80 is in service no doubt the more will become available. Regular and TA battalions have an 81mm mortar platoon and a MILAN anti-tank platoon. Since there is unlikely to be a tank threat on the British mainland, these might be redeployed to British Forces in Germany.

Night vision and perimeter protection equipment would be important tools in the business of guarding vital installations. Each infantry battalion does have both image intensification (II) equipment and intruder alarms. Also unattended ground sensors or UGS are widely used for internal security tasks in Northern Ireland and could easily be redeployed to the mainland. There are various II equipments in service. NOD (A) (The Night Observation Device Model A) is one example. It is a passive long range sight used for surveillance and artillery fire control purposes. The image intensification process makes the most of whatever ambient light there is and magnifies it thousands of times. The NOD A, for instance, is fitted with a 40mm, cascade image-intensifier tube which produces an overall luminous gain of up to 80,000

Above: 'POWs' being processed at the RAOC depot at Blackdown during Exercise 'Brave Defender'. They are in the search position. Soviet servicemen, if captured in the UK, would remain in military, not police custody.

times. Power is derived from a single 6.75 V battery. The other main use for II devices is as a weapon sight. Obviously the field of view is more limited and, because the device is smaller and lighter, the overall magnification gain is less. Nevertheless these weapon sights, several examples of which are in service with the British Army, are an extremely effective means of engaging targets at night.

Although the bulk of Royal Engineer manpower and equipment resources are allocated to the British Army in Germany, some would be available for Home Defence purposes. Engineers would be used to improve the physical defences of Key Points, for route clearance, for runway damage repair and for bomb disposal. The Royal Engineers are responsible for dealing with unexploded conventional bombs delivered by enemy aircraft while the Royal Army Ordnance Corps or RAOC are tasked to deal with explosive devices planted by Spetsnaz sabotage teams or terrorists. Perhaps the greatest engineer effort is expended on runway damage repair. The Russians would undoubtedly try to put the RAF's main air defence airfields and runways out of commission by cratering the runways. The Tornado is a remarkably versatile aircraft and, for its size, weight and capability, can take off in a relatively short space, but clearly runways that are seriously cratered will have to be repaired instantly. The Royal Engineer airfield repair regiments are able to do this. They have all the equipment and manpower needed to repair and resurface runways in a matter of hours. It will be their job to ensure that runways remain serviceable.

Infantry, whether Regular, TA or HSF, needs transport to be effective, particularly when they are responsible for large areas of countryside. There is little or no problem when it comes to vehicles. Where there are insufficient military vehicles, Dormant Hire vehicles will be used and, in the last resort, transport would be requisitioned. Air transport and support is, unfortunately, a different story. All RAF Chinook and Puma helicopters are likely to be deployed to Germany. Hercules and other transport aircraft would be airlifting men, resupplies and equipment to support BAOR as well. However, some Army Air Corps Gazelles or Lynxes may be available and RAF Gazelles used in peacetime for training would be available for liaison work. Fixed-wing training aircraft would be formed into Regional Air Squadrons, but all of these aircraft are only suitable for liaison and reconnaissance tasks. Unless civilian helicopters and aircraft were requisitioned it is unlikely that there would be sufficient air transport available to move troops great distances within the United Kingdom.

So, all in all, there might be 100,000 soldiers available for the Home Defence of the country, of which only about 25,000 would be Regular manpower. Set against the land area of the United Kingdom and the nature of the threat this is not a large number. They would have to be used sparingly, precisely and cleverly. They would have a variety of tasks:

- To seek out and destroy any enemy troops inserted on to the mainland.
- To provide guards to protect key installations (or Key Points) in conjunction with and under the direction of the civil police.
- To maintain the security of military bases.
- In certain cases to defend ports, anchorages and RN shore installations where RN manpower is insufficient.
- Again, in certain cases, to defend airfields where RAF manpower resources are insufficient.
- To guard prisoners of war.
- To operate in support of the Customs Service such as providing boarding parties (though it is hoped the RNXS would be able to do this, although they are unarmed).
- Lastly, if requested, to provide military assistance to the civil authorities (MACA) or to the civil police (MACP). MACA involves the provision of equipment and expertise, MACP the provision of military muscle if the police cannot cope unaided with any particular situation (as in Northern Ireland today).

In the final analysis, the Army is, of course, responsible for the security of the landmass of the British Isles. As we have seen, they are unlikely in the extreme to have to face invasion by a formed body of troops. But Spetsnaz can and undoubtedly would be infiltrated in a number of different ways. It would be the task of the Army to locate and destroy them as early as possible after insertion. Regional, County and TAOR commanders would be allocated a number of troops that would reflect the number of key points in their area. Clearly the counties of No. 6 Region in the south east of England, where there is a plethora of KPs, would require many more military units than Wales. But, although different commanders would be allocated varying numbers of troops, they would all have something in common – none would have enough. The resources of a small professional army will only stretch so far. Unlike France or Germany, who maintain large national service armies in peacetime and can therefore call upon large resources in wartime, Britain's military manpower resources can only be relatively meagre.

Commanders would be allocated, again depending upon the perceived threat to their area, a mix of Regular, TA and HSF units and some CGRs and GSUs. Some of these men would be available more or less immediately, namely the Regular infantry battalions and the CGRs and some would take a little longer and would not be available until the Queen's Order had been signed. This is the means by which the Government authorizes the mobilization of the TA and the Reserves. Thus the TA, HSF and GSUs would take a matter of days to call up and deploy. The Reservists would also need some refresher training. Commanders' plans would therefore have to evolve.

Right: An RNR Sailor guards HMS *Eagle* on Merseyside during Exercise 'Brave Defender'. Note the blank on the end of the barrel of his SLR rifle. This simulates the action of a live round allowing the semi-automatic mechanism of the rifle to cock the weapon automatically. It also prevents wadding from 'blank' rounds exiting from the muzzle and causing possible injury.

Initially regular infantrymen might be providing static guards for crucial KPs. As TA soldiers and reservists became available, it is most unlikely that regular soldiers would be used for static duties.

When all his forces were available, a commander would, in most circumstances, dispose of his available troops in three categories. First he would be required to provide certain static guards for KPs in his area of responsibility. Secondly he would wish to dominate the ground with mobile forces so that he could gather intelligence, deter the enemy and reassure the population. Ideally this would be done by TA reconnaissance regiments in Fox armoured cars or TA Yeomanry Regiments in Land Rovers, but might have to be carried out by infantry in military or requisitioned transport. If they were available, patrols could also be carried out by helicopter or the fixed wing aircraft of the Regional Air Squadrons. But patrolling from the air should be regarded as something that can be superimposed on ground patrolling. It is no substitute for the intimate contact with the population achieved by foot and vehicle patrolling. Thirdly, a commander – at whatever level – would always wish to maintain a Mobile Reserve, sometimes known as a Quick Reaction Force or QRF with which he could reinforce threatened areas. A static guard is always at a disadvantage; the attacker has the advantage both of surprise and of being able to concentrate his forces undetected at a point of his own choosing. Thus a small detachment guarding, for instance, a radio rebroadcast station could find itself under attack by a highly professional Spetsnaz unit armed with automatic weapons, demolition equipment and possibly stand off weapons such as the RPG-7 rocket-launcher or even a laser target marker (LTM) to guide laser guided munitions (LGM) launched from an aircraft on to the KP. In such circumstances a KP might need reinforcing quickly. In any event a prudent commander should

never be without a reserve to meet the unexpected and, having committed his reserve, he must reconstitute it by nominating another unit whose primary task is not indispensable.

The 'bread and butter' of Home Defence for the military is the business of guarding Key Points. A KP is by definition an installation the disruption or destruction of whose function would impair the national war effort. Some KPs are clearly more important than others and they are categorized to reflect their importance. The value of all KPs is limited to some extent by time and space: for instance, a communications KP might only be relevant from some stage in transition to war until some particular information had been passed through it; in the same way, if a KP is mobile (such as a Ground Launched Cruise Missile – until the INF Treaty abolishes them) the ground which it occupies is only significant while it remains there.

KPs can be large complex areas such as a port or an airfield or a communications 'aerial farm' of many acres, or they can be covert equipments in ordinary buildings such as a computer controlling some vital function or they could be underground hardened complexes with small concealed entrances. Within each KP are a number of vulnerable points (VPs) upon which the function of the KP is dependent. These can be power generators or fuel tanks or the fuel lines connecting them. Some KPs have 'tailouts' which are VP elements running outside the perimeter fence for some distance before dispersion of the vital function: for instance, a communications line running underground from a KP until it disperses into the British Telecom system, or a single track branch railway line running from an ammunition depot until it joins the main railway system. Obviously such extensions to a KP complicate the problem of guarding it.

There are various sorts of attack which a KP guard commander must contemplate. The most likely is an attempt by saboteurs to penetrate the perimeter, sabotage the vital part of the installation, probably with explosives,

Below: In a period of tension military bases and KPs would be put in a state of defence. Here soldiers are seen constructing a sentry post on the perimeter of an army base at Aldershot.

and withdraw without being discovered. Another possibility is an armed assault by a formation of troops to overpower the guard and destroy the function of the KP. The guard would have to be very weak and the Spetsnaz group exceptionally strong for this option to be attempted. A third option is the so called 'stand off' attack by a rocket launcher such as an RPG 7 or an anti tank guided weapon. This attack would be conducted from outside the perimeter and would be a relatively indiscriminate form of attack. The last option would be for a ground based team to infiltrate sufficiently close to the KP to 'mark' it from a vantage point with a Laser Target Marker (LTM). This equipment 'illuminates' a target for an aircraft launching a laser guided bomb. Provided that the bomb is launched into the LTM's 'window' it will be captured and will home on to the illuminated target.

A large KP complex might be guarded by a platoon of thirty men with perhaps a section on sentry duty at any one time, a section on patrol outside the KP to prevent a stand off attack, and a third section resting and acting as the Reserve. To complicate matters further commanders cannot patrol outside KPs until emergency legislation has been passed. Assuming it is, then the army will be authorized to patrol in Ground Defence Areas or GDAs surrounding KPs. Clearly it would be impossible to protect a KP adequately by simply sitting inside its perimeter fence. All a GDA does is to allow the Army to patrol around a KP to prevent saboteurs reaching the KP or launching a stand off attack. Britain and Denmark alone of NATO's member states do not have some permanent form of emergency power legislation.[6] In Britain, where individual liberty is held so dear, special legislation would be introduced only in the last resort.[7] If legislation were passed it would be possible to patrol outside perimeters, set up vehicle check points, protect VPs outside the perimeter and search or sweep areas where an enemy might lie up or from which a stand off attack might be launched. All this would be carried out in conjunction with the civil police.

Below: A typical KP somewhere in southern England. Installations such as these have long perimeters and require large numbers of soldiers to guard effectively.

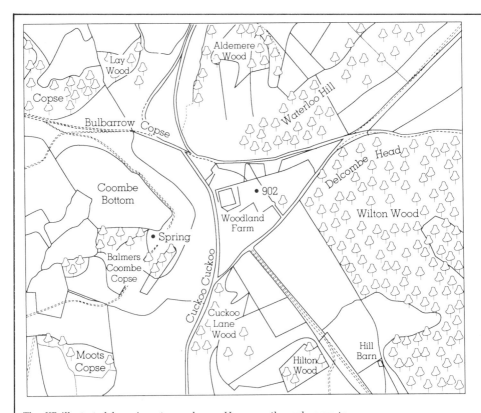

The KP illustrated here is not a real one. However the only way to bring the problems of a KP commander alive is to illustrate them on a piece of ground. KP D108 is situated in wooded downland. It stands on top of a hill near spot height 902. The KP, which is a radio relay site, is a square compound surrounded by a 7ft chain link fence. It is also surrounded by several woods, any one of which could serve as sites from which stand-off weapons would be launched at the KP. It is realistic to assume that a maximum of a platoon would be allocated to guard the site. If it were as little as a section then only the immediate defence of the VPs within the compound would be possible. But with a platoon the best way to go about the defence of KP D108 would probably be to allocate one section to the defence of the VPs within the KP and one section to patrol the GDA surrounding the KP (assuming the necessary legislation had been passed) thus preventing a stand-off attack from Wilton Wood or Cuckoo Lane Wood, both of which probably have line of sight to the KP. Land Rover patrols along Cuckoo Lane and the road to the north of the KP might be a good idea. A third section would act as reserve and QRF and, if not deployed, would be resting. Each section would complete eight hours in each role in every 24 hours. Platoon HQ would, of course, be situated in the KP.

The Section responsible for the close defence of the KP would consist of ten men. Certainly one man would be on the gate controlling access of vehicles and pedestrians. The three VPs would all have to have a double sentry guarding each one – a single man could be overpowered too easily. The section could guard two of the VPs (total four men) and

1. Entry point
2. Computer building (VP)
3. Caravan
4. Radio Relay Mast (VP)
5. Disused petrol pump
6. Hard standing
7. Derelict building
8. Generator building and office (VP)
9. Radio mast
10. 7ft Chain-link fence
11. Nissen hut

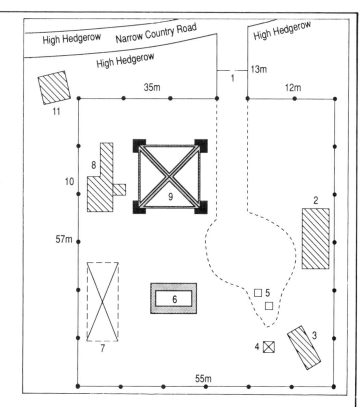

Platoon HQ base itself in the third, the computer building. A Prowler Guard of a further two men would patrol the perimeter fence thus leaving two men off duty and the section commander in a position to organize his section.

The Platoon Commander would wish to put the KP in a state of defence. He would certainly dig trenches, which the section could use in the event of a concerted attack on the KP, particularly an air attack. He might sandbag the computer and generator buildings; he could screen them with hessian, thus denying a would-be attacker with a stand-off weapon aiming mark. He could thicken up the perimeter fence with concertina wire if the stores were available. He could also install an infra-red fence or unattended ground sensor (UGS) system if either were available.

The section dominating the GDA could mount any combination of vehicle or foot patrols or standing patrols or observation posts (OPs) at likely stand-off attack or enemy OP positions or along likely approaches to the KP. To do this the Platoon Commander would have to put himself in the mind of the enemy and try to work out how he would attack the KP if roles were reversed. This would require cunning, good planning and excellent fieldcraft and would be best executed by regular or TA soldiers. Their task would be made much easier at night if they were issued with image intensifier (II) night vision surveillance and target acquisition equipment.

A platoon commander at KP D108 would be a busy man.

The Army would also be responsible for mobile operations. These would be undertaken by reserves held centrally anywhere within their area of responsibility. Apart from routine patrolling, reserves would have the capability to mount Search and Destroy or Cordon and Search operations. Search and Destroy operations, as their name implies, would involve at least a company sized unit searching a large area of countryside for an elusive and numerically small enemy force such as a Spetsnaz unit, locating it, pinning it down and destroying it. In conventional warfare the destruction of the enemy can be achieved by air power or artillery. This would not be the case in Home Defence operations, mainly because the aircraft and guns are not available, but also because such operations would be inappropriate in the United Kingdom. Therefore infantry companies or battalions would have to locate and destroy such targets using infantry weapons. Helicopters and Beagle aircraft from the Regional Air Squadrons would be an invaluable aid in Search and Destroy operations. The initial report of the presence of enemy troops in a particular location might come in the first place from a sighting from the air or more likely from a report from an alert and suspicious member of the civilian population. Aircraft might be used to verify the sighting, but troop lift helicopters would be particularly valuable to achieve surprise by flying in the troops involved in the operation. In a company sized operation, one platoon might be dropped as a 'stop line' beyond the enemy location while two other platoons could be dropped in a position from which one

Above: A Quick Reaction force disembarks from an RAF Wessex helicopter on Exercise 'Brave Defender'. Helicopters would provide one of the quickest and most effective means of moving troops in a crisis.

Above: A highly professional-looking TA Yeomanry Regiment mobile patrol mounted in a stripped down Land Rover with a GPMG on an anti-aircraft mount in the rear of the vehicle. The radio fit allows the vehicle to communicate over long distances. Patrols such as these would normally operate in pairs and would be used by County Military HQs for route reconnaissance, traffic control, radio relay and NBC recce.

could provide fire support for an assault while the other launched an assault. Provided that the time factor was not critical, such an operation could, of course, be undertaken using road transport followed by an approach on foot. Bearing in mind the likely shortage of helicopters this latter course would be the most likely.

Search and Destroy operations would not be conducted randomly or on speculation, only as a result of Intelligence. They would be carried out by Regular and TA infantry battalions and possibly CGR companies. GSU and HSF units would not be expected to carry out such complex operations.

The other likely operation to be carried out by a Reserve force would be a Cordon and Search. Such an operation is more manpower intensive than a Search and Destroy operation and is more likely to be undertaken when looking for terrorists or small parties of lightly armed men. It can often take place in an urban setting. As the term implies the operation involves throwing a cordon around a small hamlet or farmhouse or some other collection of buildings and then methodically searching the area inside the cordon. It is a complex operation necessitating very precise and detailed orders so as to ensure that everyone knows exactly where everyone else is and knows their own arcs of fire.

Reserves would have to react very quickly even to merely make contact with a Spetsnaz unit. Sightings would be fleeting and, if compromised, a Spetsnaz unit would not wait around to be destroyed. Nevertheless Search

and Destroy or Cordon and Search are the only way that the initiative can be regained from Spetsnaz. Painstaking and somewhat 'hit and miss' it might be, but occasionally such operations pay dividends as has been demonstrated in many of Britain's so called 'brush fire' conflicts around the world during the withdrawal from imperial responsibilities.

Primary responsibility for the internal security of the United Kingdom, whether in peacetime or war, remains with the police. Under common law, when requested, the armed forces are required to come to the assistance of the civil authorities, although at all times respecting police primacy in civil matters. A military commander retains command of his troops at all times, but, having responded to a request for MACP, he becomes responsible to the local police commander until such time as the police commander officially hands over operational responsibility to him. The transfer of responsibility should be for the minimum period and within the minimum area to enable effective military action to be taken. At the conclusion of the military operation, the police commander re-assumes operational responsibility. Clearly the deployment of troops on the streets of Britain in support of the civil power is a sensitive subject. There are many historical precedents[8] for the deployment of British soldiers within the United Kingdom other than the obvious recent example of Northern Ireland. In any future war it might not be necessary. If it were, it would be to support the police and with the sole aim of maintaining law and order.

Home Defence is not, in military terms, a glamorous subject. It has always been the 'Cinderella' of military priorities. Much of it involves the provision of static guards and other similar mundane tasks, but without a secure and well defended home base all other operations become impossible. However, Exercise 'Brave Defender'[9] and subsequent smaller Home Defence exercises have sparked a new enthusiasm for the whole subject. Home Defence is 'fashionable' again. It is a military fact of life that armed forces operations on mainland Britain would certainly be as significant to the outcome of a conventional war in Europe as the manoeuvres of armoured divisions on the Hanover Plain or in the Fulda Gap.

Notes:

1. Home Defence Regions are explained in Chapter 8.
2. Command, control and communications is normally referred to in the Armed Forces by the shorthand C3.
3. *See also* Chapter 1.
4. HSF Terms of Reference.
5. During Exercise 'Brave Defender' in 1985 (*see* Chapter 10) the author encountered an HSF platoon in which the platoon commander had managed to recruit two ex Warrant Officers and several ex Senior NCOs from his old battalion in which they had all served together as regular soldiers. The level of expertise in the platoon was most impressive!
6. In West Germany, emergency legislation was agreed in 1968 under the GDU/SPD Government. It provides a comprehensive list of measures that a German government can take in time of crisis including control of utilities and civil liberties. The Dutch Parliament passed similar emergency legislation in the 1984–5 session and the Norwegian Government passed a series of 'special measure for warlike situations' in1960. Legislation also exists in Canada, the USA, Belgium, Greece, Portugal, Iceland, Spain, Turkey, Italy, France and Luxemburg.
7. For a different viewpoint on GDAs *see* Duncan Campbell's article in the *New Statesman* of 6 September 1985.
8. 'Peterloo', the Sidney Street Siege, the Welsh coal miner's strike during the First World War, the Iranian Embassy Siege, troop deployments at Heathrow Airport are but a few examples in recent history.
9. *See* Chapter 10.

8. The Role of the Police in War

There are 43 police forces in England and Wales, eight in Scotland and one (the Royal Ulster Constabulary) in Northern Ireland. Each force is responsible for law enforcement in its own area, but there is constant co operation between them. In London, the Metropolitan Police Force, with its headquarters at New Scotland Yard, is responsible for an area within a radius of fifteen miles from the centre of London, but excluding the City of London where there is a separate force. The strength of the regular police force in Great Britain[1] is almost 135,000 (including nearly 12,000 policewomen); in Northern Ireland the strength of the RUC is about 8,000 plus about 5,000 full and part time reserve members.[2] The size of different forces varies tremendously and depends upon the area and the population they serve. The strength of the Metropolitan Police Force, the largest, is more than 27,000. Such a highly trained body of men would obviously be invaluable in wartime.

It is instructive to look at the part played by the police in the defence of Britain in the past. After the establishment of regular police forces in the early nineteenth century there was no war during the rest of the century which affected the police service as such. However, some policemen were recalled to the colours as reservists or joined as volunteers during the Boer War. But overt co operation with the military authorities in peacetime was frowned upon since it was considered likely to create a war scare. This fear of causing public alarm at home and arousing animosities abroad stood for a long time in the way of effective co operation between the civil and military authorities. For instance in the summer of 1910 a draft notice prepared by a Chief Constable about the requisitioning of houses and vehicles in the event of invasion got into the hands of a Liberal parliamentary candidate who made great play with it locally as Tory warmongering. Winston Churchill, who was Home Secretary, directed that the document be recalled at once and not reissued until the Chief Constable 'saw the gleam of the German bayonets'.[3]

But the need for some measures of home defence was emphasized by the Agadir Crisis of 1911 when the possibility of war with Germany seemed imminent for some weeks. There followed in 1912 a Home Office circular to all Chief Officers of Police in England and Wales giving a brief summary of 'The Duties of the Police in the Event of War'.[4] It referred to a number of points which had been the subject of earlier circulars such as the display of mobilization posters, billeting, the requisitioning of houses and vehicles, the detention of enemy merchant ships in British harbours and the possible clearance of areas threatened by invasion. It even talked about the protection of vulnerable points, the control of undesirable aliens and the guarding of wireless stations. It was emphasized that the circular was intended for the personal and confidential information of the Chief Officers themselves and called for no immediate action.

A revised version of this circular was issued on 30 July 1914 bringing up to date the summary of police duties in war as foreseen at that time. These remained unchanged for some time and seemed to work adequately throughout the First World War. A review of the wartime duties of the police was begun in the summer of 1927, but never got very far due to the reaffirmation in 1928 of the 'ten year rule', by which it was to be assumed that for the purpose of war preparations no major war was likely to occur within that period. Then in 1933, the 'ten year rule' having been dropped, a Home Office Committee was appointed 'to consider and advise on questions relating to the duties of the police in the event of war'.[5] This committee drew up a comprehensive set of Police War Instructions which were issued on 22 August 1939.[6] They formed the basis of standing instructions throughout the Second World War.

What is so interesting is that the police faced essentially the same problems and responsibilities they would be likely to be given in time of war today. They held vast lists of vulnerable points divided into two parts, List A showing the places to be protected by the police and List B for which the Defence Departments were responsible. They were responsible for the supervision of air raid precautions and, interestingly, they were made the centre of expertise for anti gas precautions. The plan was that all police – regular and auxiliary – should undertake anti gas training.

But much more important than any other consideration was what would the status of the police be in the event of the enemy effecting a landing and gaining control of some part of the country? Should they be armed and fight? Should they withdraw or should they remain with such of the civil population as might stay in enemy occupied territory? And in what circumstances, if any, should they resist by force?

The status of the police in this respect was made clear in a memorandum dated 2 July 1940.[7] Little had changed since a similar memorandum had been issued in 1915. It stated, 'The Police are not part of the armed forces of the Crown and therefore, in the event of a landing and effective occupation of an area by the enemy in force, should not use arms, or carry arms, in the occupied area.' This related to the occupation of part of the country by force. But there was a different instruction in the event of isolated parties of the enemy or of individuals whose aim might be sabotage or espionage. For this situation the instruction added: 'In the event of a landing by isolated parties who do not form part of an occupying force, and whose object is, or must be assumed to be, to attack civilians, destroy property and cause confusion or devastation, neither the police nor civilians are debarred, either by international or domestic law, from resisting and, if possible, destroying the enemy, in order to prevent them carrying out these objects.'[8] In this connection chief officers of police were reminded, in a circular of 12 May 1940, that it was entirely within their discretion to supply arms to selected members of their forces when they were engaged on particularly dangerous duties such as guarding vulnerable points and informed them that, while there could be no question of any general issue of arms to the Police, the Secretary of State would regard it as quite reasonable to provide revolvers 'on a more general scale' for constables guarding important vulnerable points, particularly in the eastern and south eastern area, or even for selected constables not engaged on this special duty.

Later in 1940 some consideration was given by the War Cabinet and the Army Council to the question of the police having combatant status and becoming part of the Armed Forces of the Crown, but this was dropped on the objections of the Commander in Chief.[9]

During the war the working relationship between the police and the military seems, on the whole, to have been very good. Senior officers from the armed forces and the police worked together at the Regional Headquarters[10] set up to cope with the threat of invasion. Thus it was agreed, for instance, that local detachments of troops should be earmarked to be at immediate call to the police; that Regions should have a Regional Reserve of troops, its disposal to be at the discretion of the Regional Commissioner of Police (who would be working with a military liaison officer) and that, in the event of a breakdown of communications a senior police officer might call on the nearest military HQ for assistance.[11] At the same time the Home Office circulated a pamphlet[12] which was for the information of troops assisting the police. It explained that their duties could include the provision of guards against sabotage, forming cordons to control crowd movements, preventing looting of damaged premises or clearing streets which had become obstructed. The pamphlet pointed out that all these tasks would be in support of the police and it summarized some of the main principles of the law regarding the obligations of soldiers and citizens, the limitations to be observed in the use of firearms in these circumstances and the citizen's (and the soldier is a 'citizen' in the eyes of the law) powers of arrest.

Instructions for the use of firearms in certain circumstances led to the purchase of large numbers of firearms by police forces. The Metropolitan Police, for instance, ordered 25,000 revolvers and half a million rounds of ammunition from the United States in 1940 and, when the bulk of the order was received in 1941, the pistols were quietly distributed to divisions though not to individual constables. To what extent the police would have actually fought we shall never know. But they had the means and would undoubtedly have done so in some limited circumstances.

It is surprising how little the situation has changed to this day. As in the Second World War, if Regional Government were established today, each Chief Constable would be responsible, through his Regional Police Commander, to the Regional Commissioner. It is planned that police forces should be grouped into regions identical with Home Defence Regions.[13] Also the Home Secretary has designated certain Chief Officers of Police to the staffs

Below: The Hampshire Constabulary Military Liaison Officer discussing operational plans with a Staff Officer from the Hampshire Military HQ during Exercise 'Brave Defender'.

of the Regional Police Commanders so that an organization could be formed in times of tension. But the Regional Police Commanders hold full time peacetime jobs and therefore they appoint a full time staff officer, normally of the rank of Superintendent, whose job it is to co ordinate the planning of police war duties and any peacetime training that might be necessary. It is this officer who keeps contingency plans up to date, briefs the Regional Police Commander (designate), and who liaises with county and military authorities. In normal circumstances it is only this one officer in each police force who is engaged in full time planning for war duties.

Police forces in the United Kingdom, although all subject to the authority of the Home Office, are independent organizations, therefore each police force is responsible for developing its own war plans. All policemen receive background instruction in civil defence early in their careers and further training does follow for most officers. Inspectors and Chief Inspectors attend regional training courses and more senior officers attend special courses run for the police at the Civil Defence College. As can be seen, the tendency is to limit serious training for war duties to higher ranking officers. There is some logic to this: by and large the duties of the policeman on the beat may not differ greatly during wartime from his peacetime duties. He will still be rendering assistance to the general public though probably at a rather more intense rate. Officers, on the other hand, will be faced with much more intractable problems of resource allocation, inadequate communications, liaison with other government and military authorities and recruiting more police manpower.

If a War Emergency developed, the Home Office – in keeping with other government departments – would issue instructions for police war prepara- tion to begin. Chief Constables would be responsible for the implementation of their own county war plans. This is the point at which all that preparatory and contingency work carried out by just one full time police staff officer would be tested. It is important to remember that at this juncture the principal peacetime responsibilities of the police – the prevention of crime, the preservation of life and property, the maintenance of law and order, the detection and detention of offenders, traffic management and helping and advising the public – would all continue and no doubt increase. The lessons of both wars show that, for the most part, policemen carried on being policemen in much the same way.

But as well as carrying on with their peacetime responsibilities and increasing, in so far as is possible, the manpower available to the police, the police authorities would implement plans for Police Liaison Officers to assume their posts at Region, County and District War Headquarters. In some cases it is also planned for police officers to be stationed at the Headquarters of other essential Services such as the Fire Service. These plans have been rehearsed in peacetime and the officers concerned would, in most cases, have met the staff of the headquarters with which they would be expected to work in wartime. If the situation deteriorated the police would be required to undertake the guarding of vital installations or Key Points (KPs). If an armed guard were required to prevent an attack by Spetsnaz, it would be provided by the military although there would always be a police presence to ensure police primacy. But in the majority of cases there is insufficient military man- power to guard every KP. Less sensitive KPs would probably only have a police guard. There are no plans to arm the police beyond the capability that the police have in peacetime to protect themselves where they face an armed threat. The sort of KPs for which the police would be likely to be responsible are police stations themselves, food and fuel stores.[14]

During a period of tension (and reinforcement of Europe) the police would have the additional task of managing traffic to ease the movement of essential supplies and services and of the armed services. They would have to ensure that the emergency services had free access to the road system and were not in any way interfered with in the carrying out of their duties. The military requirement to move large quantities of men and equipment in a relatively short time during mobilization would call for a major police commitment. Quite complex traffic management schemes would have to be implemented to ensure that military convoys reached the ports of embarkation at Southampton, Portsmouth, Dover, Ramsgate, Sheerness, Felixstowe, Harwich and Hull. The police might also be required to assist the military in securing accommodation and, under the provisions of emergency legislation, requisitioning buildings, vehicles and essential materials. Slow moving military convoys could cause traffic chaos if they were not properly managed. Although military police would control the organization of the convoy itself, it would be inappropriate for them to direct civilian traffic.

While the police were faced with this extra major task they would also find themselves responsible for warning the public of any impending air attack. Police stations house terminals for the United Kingdom Warning and Monitoring organization (UKWMO).[15] These are called carrier receiver warning points and form part of the system for warning the public of air attack and fallout. The police are also responsible for manning and operating power sirens in urban areas. During a period of tension the police would be responsible for bringing carrier receiver warning points in police stations and elsewhere to full readiness. In the event of a conventional air attack the police would be responsible for public safety and for directing the homeless or refugees to temporary accommodation and feeding centres, managing traffic in affected areas and helping the emergency services carry out their duties. They would be very, very busy. The reality is that they would probably be too busy to deal with many routine tasks.

The only way that the police would be able to cope would be by recruiting additional manpower. There are plans for retaining officers about to leave the service and for recalling recently retired policemen. Maximum use would be made of special constables who would be expected to undertake extended periods of duty, and more special constables would be recruited. Traffic wardens would be given additional responsibilities and more civilians would be recruited to carry out administrative duties so as to release as many uniformed officers as possible to carry out 'real' police work. None of this, however, could take place overnight and it is perhaps cause for some worry that the police force cannot be easily and quickly reinforced.

As well as manning the UKWMO carrier control and carrier receiver points, messages to the public via this system would have to be supplemented by the police using loudspeakers and any other means they could lay hands on to help in relaying government messages providing information to the public. The police are better equipped than most to relay information. Of course the bulk of information of national significance can be disseminated over the radio and TV networks, but the police might well be able to supplement this if necessary as well as being a useful source of local information.

The police are well equipped with telephone, teleprinter and radio networks. VHF systems are used by headquarters for mobile communications and VHF systems for personal radio networks. In most parts of the country different police forces can communicate with one another by radio. This is backed up by Telex. These police systems would be supplemented in wartime with additional systems provided by the Home Office. These would enable

Above: Reservists acting in concert with civil police in Aldershot during Exercise 'Brave Defender'. Both police and military found that the exercise was an immensely valuable opportunity to put into practice procedures which they had seldom even discussed, let alone put into effect.

police officers at the various levels of the civil defence command structure and at war headquarters to communicate with one another. For instance there is a speech only radio link between county emergency headquarters and police wartime headquarters. This is provided by the Home Office. This capability makes the police, after the Army, the most suitably equipped organization to bring some order to an emergency situation over a wide area.

After war has been declared the Army is responsible for the safe custody and administration of all those prisoners in the country entitled to prisoner-of-war status. Thus any person entitled to such status who has been arrested by the police would be handed over to military custody. It is unlikely that the police would be in a position to arrest enemy soldiers engaged in sabotage or assassination missions. They might, however – as happened during the Second World War – be in a position to arrest the aircrew of downed enemy aircraft. Wounded prisoners of war can be taken to a civilian hospital, but it would be the responsibility of the Army to guard them.

Except in the extraordinary circumstances of Northern Ireland, the police and the military seldom work together in peacetime. The police are understandably sensitive about having their civilian status in some way compromised. Unlike the Gendarmerie in France, the Federal Border guards (Bundesgrenzchutz) in West Germany or the Guardia Civile in Spain, no British police force could ever be described as in any way paramilitary. Seen in purely military terms this can only be described as a disadvantage. It is much easier to integrate the Bundesgrenschutz in Germany (who are equipped with armoured cars and automatic weapons) with the German Army than it is the British police with the British Army. Thus in Britain co operation rather than integration is the aim. Except in the event of the complete breakdown of law and order as we know it – in which case it is impossible to predict exactly what would happen – it has always been government policy that Police Primacy and the Rule of Law should prevail. Within the United Kingdom the armed forces would therefore have to continue to operate within the law and under the direction of the police. Wherever possible a policeman would accompany all formed bodies of troops in order to advise on matters of law and order and to provide a point of contact with the public. Obviously this is in ideal circumstances and there might well be many instances when there would just not be enough policemen available. But, whatever the circumstances, the Army would operate in support of the civil power. Senior police and military officers sit next to one another in county, zone and regional headquarters so they should – at least in theory – know what the other is doing. In peacetime meetings are held involving military commanders (designate), police staff officers, chief fire officers and County Emergency Planning Officers (CEPOs). And joint police/military operations were rehearsed during Exercise 'Brave Defender' in 1985.[16]

The reality of life today is that sections of all police forces throughout Britain are trained in the use of firearms, but there are no plans to arm the police force as a whole. The weapons do not exist nor are the vast majority of policemen trained to use firearms. Additional weapons could, of course, be issued to police forces in an emergency, but there is no stated policy to do this and past experience has shown that the Army is called in to deal with situations beyond the capacity of the police. A recent and obvious example was the Iranian Embassy siege in May 1982 when the SAS were called in to storm the building.

In a nutshell, the police would be used in war as a means of releasing as many soldiers as possible to carry out combatant duties. This was their role in both world wars and all the indications are that this is how they would be used in any future conflict.

Notes:

1. 'Great Britain' comprises England, Scotland and Wales.
2. Figures from Central Office of Information pamphlet 'The Police Service in Britain'.
3. Home Office File 156920/19 quoted in *The Emergency work of the Police Forces in the Second World War*, Arthur Dixon, Home Office Publication, 1967.
4. Circular dated 7 November 1912, Home Office File 227602.
5. Home Office File 700100. The Committee consisted of representatives of the Home Office including the ARP department, the Metropolitan and City of London Police and a wider representation of County and Borough Chief Constables.
6. Arthur Dixon, *The Emergency Work of the Police Forces in the Second World War*, Home Office Publication, 1967, p. 11.
7. Home Office File 700170/18, p. 100.
8. Ibid.
9. Ibid and Home Office File 700178/82.
10. *See* Chapter 3 for a description of the Regional Organization.
11. *See* circular of 28 Aug 1939 (Home Office File 700323).
12. Home Office File 700323/11.
13. *See* Chapter 3 for a description of the Home Defence Regions.
14. Some commentators have portrayed a picture of armed police at every street corner, of firing squads and all the other trappings of an armed police state in wartime in the United Kingdom. From all my research there is no evidence of any such intention. Indeed all the evidence from both world wars is that the police tried, in so far as was possible, to maintain traditional policing methods. Of course it is possible that in the event of a complete breakdown of law and order that existing firearms could be used in some circumstances, but it is much more likely that the military would be used in such a peacekeeping role, as in Northern Ireland today.
15. *See* Chapter 4 for more details on UKWMO.
16. *See* Chapter 10 for more details on Exercise 'Brave Defender'.

9. US Forces in Britain

Ⓘn the early evening of 14 April 1986 a strike force took off simultaneously from RAF Lakenheath in East Anglia and from RAF Upper Heyford in Oxfordshire. The F-111Fs from the 48th Tactical Fighter Wing based at Lakenheath and the EF-111As of the 42nd Electronic Combat Squadron at Upper Heyford were on their way to bomb Tripoli. The fighter bombers later made a rendezvous with KC-10 and KC-135 tanker aircraft from RAF Fairford somewhere off the coast of Spain before flying on to their targets in Libya. The raid was in retaliation for Libyan terrorist actions against American targets and was also an attempt to discourage any further such attacks. The American action caused a worldwide political storm and, because the British Government had allowed the aircraft to fly from British soil, the debate raged as keenly in Britain as anywhere. It is not the purpose of this Chapter to delve into the rights and wrongs of the raid. Certainly it would appear to have been effective. The incidence of Libyan inspired and perpetrated terrorism lessened after the attack. Colonel Gadaffi has continued to maintain a lower profile to this day.

Rights and wrongs apart, what the raid did do was heighten people's perception of US bases in Britain. Although styled 'RAF' bases, they are entirely American. Apart from an RAF base commander who is in effect a liaison officer, USAF bases in this country are operated by USAF personnel. The extent to which the British Government has control over their use is also the subject of controversy. An informal agreement made between Churchill and Truman in 1952 appears to form the basis of the current understanding. In a debate on the arrival of cruise missiles in the United Kingdom, in the House of Commons on 12 May 1983 Prime Minister Margaret Thatcher was able to reassure the House that 'no nuclear weapons would be fired or launched from British territory without the agreement of the Prime Minister'.[1] Less confidently Francis Pym, then Foreign Secretary, indicated that the United Kingdom 'will have a degree of say in the authorization for the use of the new systems'.[2] The precise status of US bases in Britain is undoubtedly a contentious issue which is explored in some depth in a number of books on the subject.[3] The purpose of this book is not to explore why they are here or even whether they should be here. Rather it accepts that they are here and analyses the contribution they make to the defence of the United Kingdom.

United States military aircraft have been flying from airfields in Britain since 1942. The period from June 1942 to December 1945 saw 165 installations in the United Kingdom being used by combat units of the United States Air Force. These installations were the home of 449 squadrons (including maintenance and supply).[4] American bombers flew by day against Hitler's Germany from bases in East Anglia throughout this period while the RAF bombed by night. But with the Allied victory in Europe came demobilization and then withdrawal of all US Air Force units from the United Kingdom. They were soon to return, however. In 1948, in response to the worsening situation in Berlin, the USAF initially planned the deployment of two medium bomber wings in the UK for a period of thirty days' operational training. By September of that year, at the height of the Blockade, there were ninety B 29 bombers at seven RAF stations.

Temporary duty was turned into a permanent presence when, on 1 May 1951, the US Third Air Force was activated and given the wider task of supporting and overseeing all US Air Force activities in the United Kingdom. By the end of that year the Third Air Force comprised more than 20,000 personnel operating from six bases and two large supply and maintenance depots. Since that time the USAF presence in Britain has stabilized at approximately 27,000 military personnel supported by 2,500 US civilians.

The main USAF operating bases are at Alconbury, Bentwaters/Woodbridge, Fairford, Greenham Common, Lakenheath, Mildenhall and Upper Heyford. Most of these bases operate offensive aircraft such as the 108 A-10 Thunderbolt aircraft at Bentwaters/Woodbridge or the 66 F-111F fighter bombers at Lakenheath. Their role is in support of ground forces on the Central Front or deep strike into Warsaw Pact territory. As such these bases do not contribute directly to the defence of Britain. However, the air space over these bases is defended by the Rapier Missile System (purchased from British Aerospace) and in this respect the air defence of the region is enhanced. Large numbers of the Blindfire version of Rapier already provide air defence coverage at RAF Bentwaters and Woodbridge, RAF Lakenheath and RAF Upper Heyford as well as Alconbury, Mildenhall and Fairford. Some US bases, however, contribute more directly to the defence of these islands.

Below: These F-5E Tiger II aircraft are based in East Anglia They are interceptor aircraft and, in time of war, would be integrated into the air defence of the United Kingdom. Their actual role in peacetime is to act as 'aggressor' aircraft for US pilots practising their tactics against Soviet aircraft.

RAF Alconbury is the base for the 10th Tactical Reconnaissance Wing. This consists of the 1st Tactical Reconnaissance Squadron equipped with 20 RF-4C Phantom aircraft whose role it is to provide 24 hour all weather tactical air reconnaissance support. The 95th Reconnaissance Squadron, equipped with the highly sophisticated TR-1, is also part of the 10th Tactical Reconnaissance Wing. This aircraft is a single seat, single engined tactical reconnaissance version of the US Air Force's U-2. The aircraft is equipped with a variety of sensors to provide continuously, day or night, high altitude, all weather, stand off surveillance of the battle area in support of NATO ground and air forces. With a wingspan of 103 feet, the TR-1 is able to fly at heights above 60,000 feet for more than 3,000 miles. Also at RAF Alconbury is a squadron of 19 F-5E Tiger II aircraft. These are high performance fighter aircraft designed for air to air combat. They are fitted with internally-mounted 20mm cannon and AIM-9 Sidewinder missiles. With a top speed of 1,060mph and a maximum range of 1,600 miles with external fuel tanks, they approximate in performance to the Soviet MiG-21. Their peacetime role at Alconbury is to provide so called 'aggressor' aircraft to simulate Soviet aircraft on NATO exercises. Their pilots are expert in Soviet air to air combat tactics. But in wartime it is highly likely that these aircraft would be integrated into Britain's air defence infrastructure. Although they would

remain under US command they would come under the operational control of the UK Air Defence Region. Lacking the on board radar equipment of aircraft such as the Tornado, they could be used as a second line interceptor in much the same way as the RAF Hawk. The reconnaissance data gathered by the Phantoms and TR-1 aircraft at Alconbury could also be relevant to the defence of the country. Most of the Wing's reconnaissance tasks would probably be in support of NATO ground troops in Europe, but some sorties could be flown in support of air and maritime operations over and around Britain.

RAF Fairford is situated approximately twenty miles north of Swindon. There is a large engineering organization stationed there whose task it is to provide engineering support to any additional US strategic bombers that might be forward based in Europe in time of war. But more important for the defence of Britain there are eighteen KC-135 Stratotankers at Fairford whose role it is to provide an air to air refuelling capability for NATO aircraft in the European theatre. The first deployment of KC-135A Stratotankers to RAF Fairford took place in September 1979. The aircraft are normally stationed in the United States, but are deployed to Fairford on a rotating basis for 45 days at a time. Their primary role is in support of US aircraft but they are perfectly capable of refuelling RAF aircraft if necessary. The KC-135 carries 31,200 gallons of fuel and has a range of more than 5,000 miles. They could be an important reserve asset in any air battle in Britain's air defence region.

The Headquarters of the US Third Air Force is at RAF Mildenhall in Suffolk. Most of the aircraft at this base either contribute directly or could contribute in some way to the defence of Britain. The approximately sixteen C-130 Hercules aircraft on the base provide a large part of the tactical airlift capability of the US Air Force in Europe. Also at Mildenhall are more KC-135 Stratotankers, EC-135H airborne command and control aircraft and a detachment of four SR-71 Blackbird aircraft belonging to the 9th Strategic Reconnaissance Wing of Strategic Air Command. All these aircraft, although their primary task would be in support of US forces, would be integrated with, and would provide intelligence data for NATO and more specifically for the UK Air Defence Region. British troops regularly fly in US aircraft in peacetime and the same would undoubtedly happen in time of war.[5] The SR-71 Blackbird aircraft stationed at Mildenhall would fly strategic reconnaissance missions at a height of more than 80,000 feet and at a speed of more than 2,000mph over Warsaw Pact territory.[6] The Blackbird's range is more than 2,000 miles at Mach 3 although with air to air refuelling it is limited only by the crew's endurance. The invaluable Intelligence data provided by Blackbird would be available to Britain and would be of vital importance in evaluating and monitoring any threat from Warsaw Pact airfields. Britain has no equivalent strategic reconnaissance capability.

The HH-53 Super Jolly Green Giant helicopters stationed at RAF Bentwaters/Woodbridge provide a search and rescue capability for the Third Air Force. However, they are integrated with the RAF's own search and rescue network and an RAF pilot who found himself in a survival dinghy in the North Sea might just as easily be picked out of the sea by a US helicopter as an RAF Sea King. These few US helicopters contribute in no small way to the defence of Britain in both peace and war.

There are also some US Navy and US Army's installations in Britain. Few, if any, of the Army bases can be said to be of relevance to the defence of the mainland. There is only one large Army installation.[7] The US Navy, on the other hand, maintains a considerable presence in Britain. Its largest base is at Holy Loch in Scotland. Its task is to provide operational, material and

Right: This map shows how RAF and USAF bases in eastern England together form an integrated air defence system. Both the RAF and USAF bases are defended by Rapier SAMs, and six Bloodhound SAM sites are interwoven into the air defence matrix.

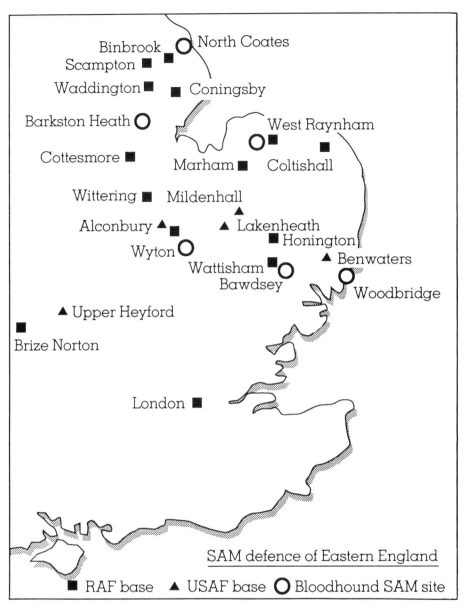

Binbrook
Scampton ■
Waddington ■ ■ Coningsby
Barkston Heath O
Cottesmore ■ Marham ■
Wittering ■ Mildenhall
Alconbury ▲■ ▲ Lakenheath
Wyton O ■ Honington
Wattisham ■O ▲ Benwaters
Bawdsey O
▲ Upper Heyford
■
Brize Norton
London ■

O North Coates
West Raynham
O■ ■
Coltishall
▲

Woodbridge

SAM defence of Eastern England

■ RAF base ▲ USAF base O Bloodhound SAM site

logistic support for nuclear powered ballistic submarines based at or visiting Holy Loch. Except in the widest strategic sense this most important of US naval bases cannot be said to contribute directly to the defence of Britain, but many of the lesser known US Navy bases do. For instance, the US Navy microwave communications link station at Thurso in Scotland operates the LORAN radio navigation system for US nuclear submarines. The facilities are jointly used by the Royal Navy.[8] Another example is the US Navy Sonar Surveillance Centre at Brawdy in South Wales. This establishment is part of the worldwide US SOSUS system which is designed to plot Russian submarine and vessel movements. Its Intelligence data would be available to HQ Eastern Atlantic Command and Channel Command, both of which NATO head-

quarters are situated at Northwood. This information would be indispensable
to the tasking of NATO naval task forces in the eastern Atlantic, in the North
Sea and particularly in the UK Iceland gap.

US Air Force and naval facilities in the UK are indisputably considerable
and they are here primarily to serve US and NATO interests in the event of
war in Europe. What is more their purpose is primarily offensive. Although
NATO is a reactive and defensive alliance, it must clearly possess a credible
offensive capability. A significant proportion of this capability is located on
NATO's 'unsinkable aircraft carrier'.[9] Thus while it would be neither credible
nor accurate to pretend that the primary purpose of US Forces in Britain is to
defend Britain's mainland, there is no doubt that a considerable degree of
defensive spin off occurs from their being here. US communications and
electronic warfare facilities, of which there are many in Britain,[10] provide
Intelligence; US Air Force bases provide reconnaissance data, an air to air
refuelling capability for RAF as well as USAF aircraft, troop lift aircraft, search
and rescue helicopters and a limited number of fighter aircraft that could be
used in the air defence role; US bases contribute to the air defence missile
coverage of the United Kingdom with their Rapier Blindfire systems; US
airfields provide alternative bases for RAF aircraft if their own bases are
temporarily out of action – and of course the reverse is true: RAF bases
provide alternative landing sites for US aircraft – the point being that the

Above: These TR-1
aircraft are based at
RAF Alconbury. Their
long range reconnais-
sance and surveil-
lance capability would
be an important
NATO asset in war.
Their capability would
also contribute to
keeping up to date the
latest assessment to
the UK Air Defence
Region.

additional US airfields in Britain add to the total number available to both RAF and USAF aircraft. Thus greater redundancy and flexibility is given to the infrastructure of the air defence of the country. Moreover, as equipment standardization increases in NATO it can only be helpful to have additional sources of US manufactured NATO equipment on Britain's mainland. A recent example of practical help provided by the USA to the RAF and Royal Navy was the provision of extra AIM-9 Sidewinder missiles for use by RAF and Royal Naval Harrier aircraft during the Falklands conflict in 1982. Finally, it is worth mentioning that the ground defence of US airfields is provided by USAF personnel and National Guardsmen flown in from the United States. It is of interest that US forces in Britain took part in 1985 in the largest Home Defence exercise ever staged on the British mainland, namely Exercise 'Brave Defender' (see Chapter 10), by mobilizing National Guardsmen in the USA and flying them to Britain.

While we are primarily concerned here with the conventional defence of the country, it should not go unmentioned that there is a small US detachment from the 12th Missile Warning Squadron stationed on the Yorkshire Moors, at Fylingdales. This is the easternmost station of the US Ballistic Missile Early Warning System (BMEWS) and is linked to a chain of similar stations in Canada and the USA. Again, its primary purpose is to provide early warning of ballistic missile attack on the continental USA, but there is some spin off

for Britain. A degree of warning – albeit limited because of the relatively short distance between missile launching sites in the Soviet Union and Britain – is provided against ballistic missile attack.

There are, of course, many much more complicated and contentious issues associated with the presence of US bases in the United Kingdom. In a nutshell the arguments in favour of a continued American presence can be summed-up in four points: the first is the coupling argument, that is to say a Russian attack on Europe would automatically involve US troops thus ensuring US participation in a 'European' war; the second is that if Britain demanded the withdrawal of US bases, she would forfeit any influence over American nuclear planning; the third argument – which makes sense to any multilater-list – is that no US bases should be sacrificed without a reciprocal and verifiable concession from the Soviet Union. The final argument in favour of the retention of US bases is that Britain derives considerable benefits from the close relationship with the US (for instance the generous access to US Intelligence and satellite facilities and to supplies of military hardware during the Falklands conflict). Since these bases enhance British and NATO security it would be foolish to endanger this relationship by demanding their removal.

Similarly, the arguments put forward against US bases in Britain can be based on four propositions: the first and most obvious is that American bases provide targets for nuclear strikes in any war in which the superpowers are involved. An extension of this argument is that by forward basing some of her offensive nuclear strike aircraft in Britain the USA would somehow be able to limit a nuclear exchange with the Soviet Union to Europe.[11] The second argument holds that siting nuclear weapons, including British ones, so near to the Soviet Union's borders is provocative and that to remove them would be to decrease international tension. This, however, ignores the fact that the conventional capability of US air bases in Britain is just as important as their nuclear role. The third argument is simply the unilateralist one, that the removal of all nuclear weapons, both US and British, would set a precedent and that to allow them to remain any longer would merely serve to enhance the value of nuclear weapons and encourage their proliferation. The weakness of this argument is that it ignores the equally important US communications and reconnaissance bases in this country and the fact that most US aircraft in Britain, such as, for instance, the 108 A-10 Thunderbolts, either do not have a nuclear role at all or, if – like the F-111s – they do, they are dual capable and have an equally important non nuclear role (as the Libyan raid demonstrated). All these assets, whether nuclear or not, would still be major targets in the event of war. The final argument against US bases in Britain is that they no longer serve the British national interest or those of Europe and that the dangers inherent in a US presence outweigh the benefits to national and NATO security.

These are the main arguments and counter arguments in a debate which has been raging ever since the USA established a sizeable presence in Britain and Europe soon after the beginning of the Cold War. Detente, the hopeful signs emanating from Gorbachev's Russia, the INF Treaty and US demands for more 'burden sharing' by her European partners have only served to add to the debate. It is the author's belief that it is in US, British and NATO interests for existing US bases to remain in Britain for the forseeable future. Of one thing there is no doubt. While they are here they do contribute indirectly to the defence of Britain, even though their main purpose is to enhance NATO's conventional and nuclear offensive capability in the European theatre.

There remains one more area of debate – the precise legal status of US forces in Britain. Their presence appears to be still based upon the informal Truman Churchill agreement of 1952[12] and the Visiting Forces Act of 30 October 1952. This latter agreement categorizes those offences that should be dealt with by the appropriate US military authority and those that should be dealt with under British law. British forces in Germany are subject to a very similar agreement. But just how much control does the British Government have over the decision to commit US forces based in Britain to battle? Unfortunately we are unlikely to discover the answer to that particular question until there is a serious clash of interests between Britain and the USA. The Prime Minister has made it perfectly clear that 'the use of these bases in an emergency would be a matter for joint decision'[13] by the British and US Governments. In the heat of an emergency could this be always guaranteed? Perhaps there is a case for a tighter definition and stricter controls. But in the final analysis, allies can only trust each other. NATO is an alliance of trust in which the United States is the dominant partner. Until the European nations of NATO are able and prepared to stand on their own feet we have little choice but to trust the senior partner.

Right: A US Air Force officer thanks British troops for their contribution to the defence of a USAF base during Exercise 'Brave Defender'.

Notes:

1. Quoted in Simon Duke's *US Defence Bases in the United Kingdom*, Macmillan Press, Oxford, 1987, from detail in House of Commons Debates for 12 May 1983 (COL 433), written answer.
2. Simon Lunn, Modernization of NATO's LRINF, Library of Congress, 31 December 1980, p. 60.
3. In particular in Simon Duke's *US Defence Bases.*
4. Quoted in brief supplied by US Third Air Force.
5. The author commanded a British Infantry battalion, the 2nd Royal Green Jackets, on an exchange exercise in 1980 at the home of the US Army's 101st Airborne Division at Fort Campbell, Kentucky. The Division's 485 helicopters were available for the battalion's use. It is standard practice for NATO troops to use all NATO aircraft.
6. Technical, operational and performance data all obtained from Third Air Force brief provided to the author.
7. This is at Burtonwood and is an Army *Matériel* Command Depot consisting of pre positioned munitions and equipment for US military reinforcements for Europe.
8. Information supplied by Captain Jerry Pape of US Naval Authority (Grosvenor Square) quoted in Simon Duke's *US Defence Bases*, p. 209.
9. This phrase is the title of a book by Duncan Campbell published by Michael Joseph, London, 1984.
10. Simon Duke (*see* Note 3) lists on page 204 19 USAF communication facilities in the United Kingdom.
11. This is an imprecise and vague argument. How a nuclear exchange could be geographically and quantitatively limited in this way is hard to imagine.
12. This agreement was reached when Churchill visited Truman in Washington in January 1952. The Americans resisted publication of the Agreement and it remains classified to this day. The communiqué issued at the end of the visit read: 'Under arrangements made for the common defense, the United States has the use of certain bases in the United Kingdom. We reaffirm the understanding that the use of the bases in an emergency would be a matter for joint decision by His Majesty's Government and the United States Government in the light of the circumstances prevailing at the time.' (State Department Bulletin, vol. 26, No. 656, 21 January 1952, p. 83; quoted in article by Dr David Gates, 'American Strategic Bases in Britain: The Agreements Governing their use', Comparative Strategy, vol. 8, No. 1 (1989)). The Churchill Truman agreement was in turn based upon the 'Spaatz Tedder' agreement of June 1946 between General Carl Spaatz of the US Air Force and Air Marshal Tedder of the RAF which provided for the use of RAF landing facilities in England for US aircraft 'for the execution of US emergency plans' (quoted in Appendix 1 of Simon Duke's *US Defence Bases, see* Note 3).
13. *See* Note 1.

10. Exercise 'Brave Defender', 1985

Exercise 'Brave Defender' took place from 6 to 13 September 1985. It was Britain's largest Home Defence exercise for forty years and involved the deployment of some 65,000 soldiers, sailors, marines and airmen. It brought the whole subject of Home Defence to the forefront of public debate. There had been large scale exercises involving BAOR in Germany on several previous occasions, the most recent being the 1984 Exercise 'Lionheart' which had involved the movement of 57,000 UK-based Regulars, TA and reserve soldiers to Germany. But, not since the Second World War, had the defence of Britain been rehearsed on a large scale.

Below: Reservists undergoing the necessary documentation before being dispatched to their assigned units on Exercise 'Brave Defender'.

Planning for Exercise 'Brave Defender' started in May 1983 with the decision by the Commanders in Chief to stage the event. It was decided that it would concentrate on the conventional ground defence of Britain and for the first time the US Forces in the country would be invited to join the exercise. It was planned that the exercise should take place in two phases. There would first, however, be a preliminary period from 2 to 6 September during which the Army would set up the logistic support for the exercise and the Enemy and Umpire Control Organization in each District throughout the country. An early objective was for there to be a large enough enemy force to make the exercise realistic. The aim was for enemy forces to consist of about two battalions in each military district. This would not have been possible without the help of BAOR which, as a quid pro quo for the help UKLF gave during Exercise 'Lionheart' in 1984, sent 110 umpire teams and eight companies of 'enemy' troops fully equipped with weapons, radios and vehicles.

In Phase 1, from 6 to 8 September, all three Services were to mobilize and deploy their Home Defence forces. During this phase, which was a weekend, the Royal Naval Reserve and HSF participants could conduct and complete their defence of Key Points and return to work on the Monday. In Phase 2, from 9 to 13 September, the exercise was to concentrate on three main themes: the defence of Key Points and their associated Ground Defence Areas, the reinforcement of Key Points by Reserves and, lastly, the deployment and committal of 5 Airborne Brigade.

The part played by volunteers in the exercise was significant. Of the total of more than 65,000 participants, 15,000 were volunteers (12,000 from the Army, 2,500 from the Royal Navy and the Royal Marines and 500 from the RAF). US Forces also deployed to guard its tactical fighter complex at RAF Bentwaters/Woodbridge as well as its logistic depot at Burtonwood near Liverpool. There was widespread police participation throughout the country although, because 'Brave Defender' was essentially a Home Defence rather than a Civil Defence exercise, their involvement was limited principally to liaison at HQs and to practical help and advice on points of law at Exercise Key Points. The Army was particularly keen to demonstrate the principle of Police Primacy.

The exercise started in earnest with a flurry of activity on Friday 7 September. After work on Friday employers all over the country were asked to release men taking part in the exercise. Some of the volunteers, mostly

HSF, would only participate for that weekend though other TA soldiers and reservists took a week off work. Reservists reported to army barracks that evening or on the Saturday morning where they were issued with additional clothing and equipment. TA soldiers got themselves to their drill halls as quickly as they could. There was a sense of urgency. It may have only been an exercise, but all over the country volunteers knew that this was no ordinary training weekend and that, for once, they were the centre of media attention. 'Brave Defender' was the first exercise in which the newly expanded Territorial Army had been given such a high profile. In March 1984 the then Minister of Defence, Michael Heseltine, had announced a major expansion and re equipping of the Territorial Army. Numbers were to be increased from 75,000 to 86,000 by 1990.[1] The TA is excellent value for money, the annual cost of a TA soldier being about 20 per cent of that of a Regular soldier. Not surprisingly the recruiters were keen to capitalize on 'Brave Defender' and a national advertising campaign was run.[2] The Press coverage was also considerable. In the national Press alone there were more than fifty separate articles on 'Brave Defender' over a period of about two weeks. There were many 'in depth' articles, particularly in the *New Statesman* and *Guardian* questioning the so called 'War Laws' and putting the view that civil rights would be sacrificed to British and US military priorities in time of war. Duncan Campbell, author of *The Unsinkable Aircraft Carrier* and other

BRAVE DEFENDER DAY BY DAY

P	reliminary period Monday 2nd September to Friday 6th September	The Army sets up the basic organisation of the exercise based on Army Districts. The enemy is br Umpires are organised.
P	hase I Friday 6th September to Sunday 8th September	All Services mobilise for the exercise. Key Point guards are assembled, trained and deployed. The Reserve and the new reserve force, the Home Service Force, are taking part only during this week
P	hase II Monday 9th September to Wednesday 11th September	Key Point defence continues to be exercised, and reinforcement with Mobile Reaction Forces is
F	inal Phase Thursday 12th September to Friday 13th September	Brave Defender is concluded with major exercises on Military Training Areas to practise dep reserves.

HOME DEFENCE – THE NEW CONCEPT BEING TESTED BY BRAVE DEFENDER

° Tri-Service
° Within the law – no emergency powers
° Based on the defence of Key Points

1. Enemy
2. Enemy
3. Enemy
4. Enemy
5. Unexpl
6. Key Po
7. GDA –
Home I
8. Mobile
to Key
9. RN Hoi
10. Protect

books questioning the US military presence in the UK, became the scourge of the MOD.

The bulk of the Press coverage was sympathetic and accurate. Articles tended to focus on certain aspects of the Exercise: an article in *The Observer* highlighted the Territorial Army and 'its force of eager volunteers who will play a key role in Exercise "Brave Defender".' The aim was to dispel the myth that there was anything sinister about Home Defence. It is an accepted part of life in every other European country – whether neutral, NATO or Warsaw Pact – why should it not be so in the United Kingdom? After all what could be more natural and sensible than the need to prepare for the defence of the homeland? It is the right of every nation to do so. And indeed, for the most part, the Press, radio and television agreed with these sentiments. As always there was a minority that tried to identify some sinister plot to undermine the

Above and right: This is part of an information booklet issued to participants in and spectators of Exercise 'Brave Defender'. The MoD PR machine went into top gear during and in those days leading up to the Exercise in order to explain to as wide a section of the

freedom of the individual. But such voices were few and far between. Thus 'Brave Defender' became a real opportunity to inform the nation about the complexities of and the requirement for Home Defence.

It was very much a tri service exercise though inevitably the Army was more involved than the other two services. In the case of the Royal Navy, 2,000 Regular sailors were responsible for the defence of naval KPs and the prevention of infiltration from the sea into certain ports and anchorages. In addition, 2,000 members of the Royal Naval Reserve (RNR) and RNXS took part in Phase 1 of the Exercise during the first weekend. RNR volunteers defended KPs and the RNXS served on board auxiliary craft and guarded Port HQs. The Royal Marines provided 2,500 Regulars and 700 men from the Royal Marines Reserve for KP defence. Clearly it is the first responsibility of the Royal Navy to man its ships during wartime, but there would be manpower

BRAVE DEFENDER – THE PARTICIPANTS

ho is taking part?
All three Services, both regular and reserve. New
forces, such as the HSF, on their first exercise.

CE	TYPE AND DESCRIPTION	ROLE	NUMBERS
Marines and Reserves ety of ports, anchorages und installations.	Royal Navy Regulars.	Defence of Naval Key Points and prevention of infiltration from sea.	2000
	Royal Naval Reserve Trained volunteers who meet the Navy's additional needs in an emergency.	Take Part in Phase I only, being trained and practising defence of Key Points.	2000
	Royal Naval Auxiliary Service A uniformed volunteer organisation of both men and women.	Take part in Phase I only. They serve on board auxiliary craft and guard Port HQs.	
	Royal Marines Regulars.	Key Point defence and Mobile Reaction Forces.	2000
	Royal Marines Band Service Bandsmen deployed throughout the Naval Service in peacetime.		500
	Royal Marines Reserve A Volunteer reserve force based on local centres. Used in war as commandos and in Home Defence.	Patrol of Key Points only	500
	Royal Fleet Reserve Royal Marines who have completed service but have 3 year reserve commitment.	Key Point defence only	200
vides the majority of for the exercise, which eir Districts. The Army s and briefs the enemy	Regulars Some units have regulars and reservists in company-sized groups.	Key Point defence, Mobile Reaction Force and elements of enemy force.	22 000
	Territorial Army (TA) The main army reserve. Locally-based volunteers with own permanent staff.	Key Point defence and Mobile Reaction Force.	7000
	Home Service Force (HSF) A new volunteer reserve force of men aged 20–50. Created to defend KPs and release regulars and TA for other roles.	Training and mobilisation during Phase I only Limited to Key Point defence.	2500
	Regular Reserve Regulars who complete less than 12 years service, complete up to 12 years in Regular Reserve.	May volunteer to take part in peacetime exercises.	2500
	British Army of the Rhine (BAOR) Regulars from units based in West Germany.	Troops assigned to BAOR are providing part of the enemy – and are also providing 110 team of umpires to help control the exercise.	1000
rce AF Key Points and RAF ground defence. my air attack	RAF aircrew, ground staff and RAF Regiment Regulars.	Practice of RAF ground defence techniques, guarding Key Points and providing a network of liaison officers and some command elements to Districts. Home Defence air support is coming from at least one regional air squadron and a minimum of two helicopters per District are being used.	23 000
	Royal Auxiliary Air Force A new force still being formed around RAF stations that administer them.	Defence of airfields.	500
es Forces st time US forces have ed into UK Home	3rd Air Force US Army	Defence of selected US installations.	1000

8

EXERCISE TROOPS

The total number of more than 65,000 service personnel on Exercise 'Brave Defender' is broken down in the table below. This number includes figures for the enemy forces, for the umpire organization and the command and control organization for the exercise.

		Sub-Total	Total
ROYAL NAVY	Regulars	2,000	
	RNR 7 RNXS	2,000	4,000
ROYAL MARINES	Regulars	2,500	3,200
	RMR	700	
ARMY	Regulars	23,000	
	TA	7,000	
	HSF	2,500	35,000
	Reservists	2,500	
ROYAL AIR FORCE	Regular	23,000	
	R Aux AF	500	23,500
US FORCES	US 3rd Air	1,000	1,000
	Force and Army		
TOTAL			66,700

Left: General Sir James Glover, C-in-C UKCF, during Exercise 'Brave Defender'. Now retired, Glover had a distinguished career in the Army commanding a battalion in the Royal Green Jackets and later becoming Commander Land Forces in Northern Ireland.

remaining from training and shore establishments to guard the most important naval KPs and this was demonstrated in 'Brave Defender'.

The Army provided by far the largest number of men for the Exercise including all the 'enemy' forces and Umpire Teams. The 23,000 Regulars taking part included the 1,000 men from BAOR who provided part of the enemy and all the umpires. The remainder were used for KP defence and as mobile reaction forces. The 7,000 TA men were also used in this role though, because they had to report for duty and deploy, there was a limited delay before they could be included in the Order of Battle. This, of course, was entirely realistic since the calling out of the TA is dependent on the signing of the Queen's Order. The 2,500 HSF volunteers took part in Phase 1 only and their participation was limited to KP defence which was realistic. And finally, a limited number of reservists were called up from the much larger number that volunteered. It was deemed that 2,500 would be sufficient to test the system and, anyway, this was all the budget for the Exercise allowed. All ex-Regulars who have served less than twelve years in the Army are committed to serve the balance of those twelve years on the Reserve. In many ways this experiment of calling up Reservists was one of the most important aspects of the exercise. In any war they would be vital to make up the numbers of a small professional army. The experiment had been tried only once before during Exercise 'Lionheart', the BAOR reinforcement exercise the previous year. The aim was to build on the success of that experiment and practice the business of contacting a Reservist at his home or place of work, providing instructions as to where he should report and when, receive him, go through all the necessary documentation, provide him with clothing and equipment and finally train him to bring him back up to the standard that he had reached when he left the Regular Army some years previously. For most Reservists it was a rewarding and enjoyable experience. They were formed into GSUs and also guarded KPs.

A total of 23,000 RAF aircrew, ground staff and RAF Regiment Regulars took part in the Exercise. They practised the ground defence of airfields, guarded RAF KPs and provided liaison officers and staff for District HQs. A realistic number of aircraft were provided from at least one Regional Air Squadron and a minimum of two helicopters per district were assigned for liaison and surveillance duties. 500 men of the Royal Auxiliary Air Force practised their wartime role of defending airfields. The Royal Auxiliary Air Force is still in the process of being formed. It is a new concept for the RAF: like the Territorial Army, it is recruited locally and employed at a local airfield. For the Army this is nothing new: regiments of both the Regular and Territorial Army have been recruited and often based locally for centuries. The RAF, a twentieth century creation, was faced with a different challenge. The best answer to its requirements was to create one service within which all ranks could move freely from posting to posting, unrestricted by regimental ties and bonds. That is still the case for all Regulars in the RAF. But for the fledgling Royal Auxiliary Air Force part time volunteers it makes a lot of sense for their wartime tasks to be local. It makes training easier and it allows RAF stations to identify even more closely with the local community.[3]

Foreign nationals also took part in Exercise 'Brave Defender'. The US Third Air Force and US Army contributed 1,000 men who guarded two US bases, but there were also observers from fourteen nations who exercised their right under the Helsinki Accord to watch the exercise. Under the provisions of the Helsinki Final Act, signed in 1975, 35 nations undertook to notify one another at least 21 days in advance of their major military manoeuvres involving more than 25,000 troops, as a means of strengthening confidence and thereby contributing to increased stability and security in Europe. Signatories also undertook, on a voluntary and bilateral basis, to invite one another to send observers to attend military manoeuvres.[4]

In all there were 67,200 participants in Exercise 'Brave Defender'. They were all meticulously briefed. One brochure issued to all troops stated bluntly that 'Brave Defender' 'is to practise the defence of Britain – not to spoil the countryside or irritate local people. Participants must remember they may be using private land. Permission to use this land will have been obtained by the military authorities. Only this land may be used. If in doubt CHECK. One of the fundamental Home Defence concepts is that of *police primacy* – that is that military Home Defence takes place within the law and in support of the civil police. The police will have a liaison role in the exercise. If a police officer asks you to do something – DO IT!'[5] There was no shortage of instructions. They stated that civilian movement must not be restricted, fences and hedges must not be climbed, gates must be shut, arrable crops, farmhouses and outbuildings were out of bounds, urban areas were to be avoided, timber must not be cut, sites occupied by troops must be cleared of all refuse when vacated . . . the list of do's and don'ts went on for pages. By and large the rules were heeded. There were, of course, mistakes. A report in the *Sunday Express* on 15 September printed the alarming headline 'War Game Soldiers Fire at Family'. Only at the end of the report did it mention that the soldiers had fired blank rounds. The family had been motoring along a road owned by the MOD but to which the public had access. Soldiers were guarding a nearby Royal Naval Ammunition Depot and, when the car refused to stop having been waved down, they opened fire assuming the occupants were Exercise Spetsnaz troops. As a military spokesman said after the event, 'The Russian Special Forces will not drive up to a road block in a jeep with a hammer and sickle on the bonnet. They will be disguised as members of the local community.' Nevertheless it was an unfortunate incident. But one cannot blame the soldiers who were following their orders. Perhaps the fault lay with the exercise organizers for not closing the road.

In Gloucestershire two golfers were surprised to discover a fully armed soldier on the course, asked what he was doing and were promptly arrested as suspected enemy infiltrators. An unfortunate 19 year old shop assistant turned up at the front gate of RAF Benson to pick up a pair of trousers from his sister and was arrested and questioned for an hour. His arrival had coincided precisely with an exercise in which two servicemen in civilian clothes had been instructed to attempt to gain entry into the airfield.

Other civilians offered practical help to troops, none more wholeheartedly than the members of a grouse shoot near Darlington who offered to disperse a group of peace protesters who were taunting sentries. The 'protesters' saved themselves by disclosing their true identity as *agents provocateurs* planted by the Army.

Those soldiers who were given a brief to annoy, distract or confuse participants in the Exercise played their parts with relish. One Staff Sergeant, acting as a drunken Scot, took the opportunity to deliver abuse at a two star General he encountered at a North Yorkshire barrack gate. Another soldier was sufficiently convincing as a green and gold haired punk rocker, with earrings and 'bovver' boots, for police to arrest him for using foul language in public.

The KPs that were guarded by most participants were, in the majority of cases, not real KPs but suitable establishments or buildings on MOD property. This avoided having soldiers taking part in mock battles in the public domain thereby making a thorough nuisance of themselves and, at the same time, it

Above: Reservists to form General Support units (GSOs) arrive at Furwood Barracks, Preston for kitting out and documentation during Exercise 'Brave Defender'. These men got back into the swing of military life remarkably quickly.

avoided drawing attention to real KPs. Whereas on MOD property a greater degree of realism could be achieved and GDAs around KPs could be simulated. Unlikely locations became KPs for the purposes of the Exercise; typical of many was a First World War fortress overlooking the Solent near Portsmouth and once housing large coastal batteries commanding the entrance to the naval base. When a platoon from a Hampshire based CGR took it over it was in a chronic state of dilapidation, the fortress having been disused since the Second World War. To the amazement of the police constable who was attached to the platoon throughout their occupation of the coastal fort, the young recruits from the Light Division Depot at Winchester[6] set about making the building impregnable. They had been told that 'enemy' special forces would probably attempt to penetrate the perimeter to destroy the 'vital coastal radar' which they were guarding. Concertina wire was erected around the perimeter, trip flares were set, even tin cans were hung on the wire in the hope that any intruders might alert the defenders by making them clang if they disturbed the wire. Machine guns were sited to fire over open ground, particularly the beach, and sentries manned the barrier at the only road into the fort. Trenches were dug and disused rooms in the fort were turned into sleeping accommodation, a cookhouse and a store. The Platoon Commander commandeered a room at the top of the fort which was probably a disused Second World War lookout post. It gave him a superb view of his area of responsibility. The KP was attacked later on during the Exercise and the umpires judged that the defenders had successfully frustrated the enemy's efforts to destroy it.

In some cases real KPs were guarded. These were military KPs on military land. This was an opportunity for commanders to familiarize themselves with the real problems associated with one of the complexes that they would be responsible for in war. As a result of the Exercise real contingency plans were updated and improved in the light of the lessons learned.

Mobile Reaction Forces and Reserves were deployed to reinforce KPs under threat and to mount Search and Destroy missions. In Hampshire one such exercise was mounted from a Royal Naval Air Station on the Solent. 'Intelligence' had been received that a large Spetsnaz unit had been located on the Isle of Wight. Two companies of Regular troops from the 1st Battalion The Royal Greenjackets (1 RGJ) stationed at Tidworth and one CGR composed of recruits from The Light Division Depot, under the command of the Commanding Officer of 1 RGJ, were tasked to locate and destroy this enemy force which (it so happened) were thought to be hiding in the middle of the only training area on the Isle of Wight.

One Company was transported across the Solent by military landing craft stationed at the military port at Marchwood near Southampton. These soldiers were scheduled to hit the beach to the north of the enemy while the other company and the CGR were flown by Chinook helicopters on to the south-east and south west flanks of the enemy position. The combined force carried out a search and destroy mission soon after dawn. The operation was painstakingly slow. Looking for six men in an 800 acre wooded training area is not an easy task. The operation was complete by about midday and the troops were flown back to the mainland only to be redeployed to another operation in the north of the county, this time by 4 ton truck.

The climax of 'Brave Defender' was a parachute drop by elements of 5 Airborne Brigade at Thetford in Norfolk on 13 September. This represented the commitment of the only strategic reserve available to the then Commander in Chief UKLF, General Sir James Glover. In reality it is unlikely that any troops would be deployed by parachute within the United Kingdom. It would be more practical and efficient to fly them in RAF Hercules aircraft to whatever part of the country they were needed. However, a parachute drop made a suitable 'high profile' event for the NATO and other observers attending the Exercise.

So every aspect of Home Defence was rehearsed. What were the lessons of this unprecedented Exercise? There were many. Even though MOULD, when it is completed, will be a vast improvement on anything that has existed before, communications often fall short of the ideal. A comprehensive military communications network would almost certainly be prohibitively expensive. Much use was made, and will probably have to continue to be made, of British Telecom telephone boxes. Certainly Home Defence communications are adequate and many lessons were learned on how to make the best use of what is available.

The second important lesson was the confirmation – if it was needed – that the TA, the HSF and the Reserves are more than capable of defending KPs. While this was probably assumed for the TA, it was very much a test for the HSF and Reservists. Both passed the tests with flying colours.

Another important lesson was the value of liaison. Home Defence involves the co ordination of central government, local government, voluntary organizations, the police, the fire service, the health authorities, the Royal Navy, the Royal Air Force and the Army as well as other smaller organizations. Most of these agencies are independent. 'Brave Defender' enabled them to work together and to refine procedures. Much of this process was helped by close liaison and the actual stationing of liaison officers in one another's headquarters.

Of course, much was learned about defending KPs. The degree of vulnerability of many real KPs was reassessed in the light of experience and

Right: Regular soldiers erecting a POW cage at Aldershot in Hampshire during Exercise 'Brave Defender'. 'Enemy' POWs were used to practise Regular and TA troops in the processing and handling of POWs. Notice the novel idea of using the tennis court perimeter fencing as the inner perimeter of the POW cage.

Right: General Sir Geoffrey Howlett, then Commander South East District, talking to 'Orange Force' soldiers taken prisoner during the exercise. These men were put through the motions of the processing and documentation necessary for all POWs. They were then 'recycled' to live again as 'enemy' troops.

practical steps have been taken since 1985 to reduce that vulnerability. Some of these lessons were the direct result of reports and recommendations written by KP Guard Commanders in their post Exercise reports. As funds become available, blast proof walls and other improvements will be made to important KPs.

Helicopters proved an indispensable asset in the movement of local reserves around counties and strategic reserves around the country. Whether or not the numbers of RAF support helicopters available for Exercise 'Brave Defender' were realistic, taking into account that their primary role is likely to be with BAOR, is questionable. However, the Exercise confirmed the need for these helicopters and it is likely that the necessary arrangements will be made to hire civilian helicopters in a time of emergency in much the same way as British Airways jets would be used to reinforce Europe.

The main lesson of the Exercise – and this was no surprise – was that there are insufficient troops available to carry out the Home Defence role

Right: Reservists receiving instruction in the firing of the SLR on Exercise 'Brave Defender'. Firing a rifle accurately is rather like riding a bike. Men who were capable shots when they were regular soldiers found that it was relatively easy to recapture 90 per cent of their previous expertise after only half an hour's instruction.

comprehensively. As a result a review was set in hand to look at better ways of deploying the 148,000 Reservists available more quickly and more efficiently so that more Regular and TA troops can be used as mobile reaction forces and reserves. Quite often during 'Brave Defender' a county reserve was reduced to one company of infantry (about 100 men). This was, in most cases, clearly inadequate to meet a likely emergency. It is hoped that a reallocation of wartime reservists will release sufficient Regular and TA soldiers to form at least one additional infantry brigade for mobile tasks. This would be invaluable.

The impetus provided by 'Brave Defender' has ensured that Home Defence retains a high profile. Just before Parliament rose for its summer recess on 28 July 1988, the Armed Forces Minister, Ian Stewart, announced that there would be nine separate Home Defence exercises throughout Great Britain from September to November 1988, covering all the military districts except Northern Ireland. In his written statement to the House of Commons, Mr Stewart stated that the purpose of these exercises 'will be to test our plans for a wide range of Home Defence operations. It is useful to exercise these plans at a period when international tension is low, so as to maintain effectiveness and to ensure that, if the need arose, they could be operated successfully in transition to war. The military personnel involved in each exercise will be practising their task of defending installations in the UK – including in a few cases ports, airfields and other operational facilities . . .'[7] One of these exercises was Exercise 'Strong Link 88'. Unlike 'Brave Defender', 'Strong Link' was confined to the five counties – Cumbria, Lancashire, Merseyside, Greater Manchester and Cheshire – which form the Army's North West District. The District also includes the Isle of Man where exercises

Left: Paras drop at Thetford in Norfolk. The drop was the climax of the Exercise and was watched by attachés and military representatives from all over the world. The drop was designed to demonstrate the capability to insert a large reaction force anywhere in the UK. Whether in reality this would be done by parachute rather than by air landing is another matter but the event was a suitable 'high profile' climax to Exercise 'Brave Defender'.

Left: A member of 6 Company, 5 Royal Anglians (an HSF Company) defending a KP on Exercise 'Brave Defender'. He is armed with an SLR and equipped with a personal radio and binoculars. Note that he has removed the cap badge from his beret to aid his personal camouflage.

were conducted for the first time since the Second World War. It was a very small exercise by the standards of 'Brave Defender': as well as 3,000 Regular, TA and reserve troops, elements of the Royal Navy, Royal Marines Reserve, RAF, the US Army, local police forces and other civil agencies took part. Again the majority of troops were deployed to defend vital installations such as Manchester International Airport, Seaforth Docks in Liverpool, communication centres and armament depots, from attacks by enemy sabotage teams while others formed mobile reaction forces. More than two dozen KPs throughout the region were defended during 'Strong Link'.

Additional realism was provided at the beginning of the Exercise by the off loading of ammunition from the NATO armaments depot at Broughton Moor near Workington in Cumbria to the US Navy replenishment ship *Savannah* anchored offshore which was taking part in the NATO naval exercise 'Teamwork 88'. Troops escorted the RN vehicles carrying the ammunition to Workington Docks which they secured while the ammunition was loaded on to civilian ships which transferred it to the *Savannah*. The Exercise continued with the mobilization of TA and HSF units to take over the defence of KPs. One KP, though, was defended by US troops – the US stores depot at Burtonwood – where an enemy team infiltrated the rear of the base and sabotaged a goods train. Army bomb disposal teams, the local fire brigade and ambulance teams were called out to provide assistance.

The final phase saw two companies of the 1st Battalion The Cheshire Regiment and two companies from the 4th King's Own Border Regiment, the latter a TA unit, flying to the Isle of Man in RAF Hercules aircraft to track down 'enemy infiltrators' on the island. Working with the island's uniformed volunteer civil defence unit and Royal Navy reservists manning the minesweeper HMS *Ribble* and the patrol boats HMS *Striker* and HMS *Biter*, the soldiers conducted search and destroy operations until the Exercise ended. 'Strong Link' and the other small exercises held in the autumn of 1988 put into practice many of the lessons learned during 'Brave Defender'.

'Brave Defender', the most ambitious Home Defence Exercise to take place since the end of the Second World War and costing in the region of £3 million, was judged a success. A lot went wrong but that is what exercises are for. Only in one major respect was the exercise unrealistic. The reinforcement of Europe and the Defence of the Nation were not exercised together: 'Lionheart' took place in 1984, 'Brave Defender' in 1985. The ultimate test of the ability of the armed forces to mobilize to reinforce BAOR while simultaneously deploying to defend the Home Base has not yet been undertaken. Another national Home Defence exercise is planned for the early 1990s. Whether or not it will take place at the same time as a reinforcement of BAOR is yet to be announced. Many await the announcement with interest.

Notes:

1. This programme is well under way with new battalions forming and recruiting to schedule.
2. One of these depicted a platoon of smiling TA soldiers with the words 'Thank you' superimposed over the photograph. Written below were these words: 'The Territorial Army extends its thanks to Britain's employers. The Territorial Army extends its heartfelt thanks to all those employers, large and small, who allow their employees to participate in Territorial Army training – particularly those who took part in Exercise "Brave Defender" last week. Without your co operation we would not have been able to carry out an exercise of vital importance to Britain and NATO. As you may already know, the Territorial Army makes up one third of the nation's land forces. And we're expanding. Our role, in the event of war, would be to fight alongside the Regular Army. So you can appreciate how crucial it is for us to spend our spare time training up to their standards. Most of this work is done during weekday evenings and at weekends, but we also need to carry out full scale exercises. Last year it was the highly successful Exercise 'Lionheart' in Germany. This year 'Brave Defender' in Britain.

    Naturally we believe the Territorial Army exists to serve the nation in the broadest sense. But we also know, from talking to employers, that many of you benefit directly from the kind of experience and training that the Territorial Army gives to your employees.'
3. Royal Auxiliary Air Force Squadrons currently formed are:
    2503 (County of Lincoln) Field Squadron
    2620 (County of Norfolk) Field Squadron
    2622 (Highland) Field Squadron
    2623 (East Anglian) Field Squadron
    2624 (County of Oxford) Field Squadron
    2625 (County of Cornwall) Field Squadron
4. The 35 Signatories of the Helsinki accord were: Austria, Belgium, Bulgaria, Canada, Cyprus, Czechoslovakia, Denmark, Finland, France, FRG, GDR, Greece, Hungary, Iceland, Ireland, Italy, Lichtenstein, Luxemburg, Malta, Monaco, Norway, Netherlands, Poland, Portugal, Roumania, San Marino, Spain, Holy See, Sweden, Switzerland, Turkey, UK, USA, USSR, Yugoslavia. The following countries sent observers to the Exercise: Austria (2), FRG, Finland, Greece, Ireland (2), Italy (2). Norway, Portugal (2), Spain (2). Sweden (2), Switzerland (2), Turkey, Yugoslavia, USA.
5. UKLF instructional pamphlet to troops taking part in Exercise 'Brave Defender' 1985.
6. The Author was commanding officer of the Light Division Depot at the time.
7. Quoted in *Armed Forces* magazine, December 1988, vol. 7, No. 12.

11. The Future

We stand at a crossroads as far as Home Defence is concerned. The first duty of any government is to ensure the security of the homeland. Yet, because of our international defence com mitments both within and outside NATO, some aspects of our home defence are inadequate. Our principal naval bases and some of our military airfields remain unprotected by air defence missiles. The Territorial Army and Home Defence Forces are inadequate in numbers and not equipped both to defend key installations in Britain as well as reinforce Germany. It is by no means certain that we possess an adequate minesweeping and offensive mining capability to protect the strategic deterrent and ensure that our larger ships have access to their bases. Obviously it would be preferable to retain balanced forces ready to meet whatever crisis might face the country, but, as the cost of defence rises exponentially, that is no longer possible. We have to specialize to some extent while at the same time playing our full part in NATO. With withdrawal from Hong Kong in 1997 and the possible withdrawal from other outposts of Empire in the forseeable future, resources may become available for Home Defence. Also, with balanced conventional arms reductions looking increasingly likely in Europe, it may be possible to reduce the strength of BAOR. The international scene is changing so fast at present that it is difficult to be more specific than this. But there is so much in the melting pot that resources are likely to be released in the relatively near future. They should be redeployed to Home Defence. When we are confident that the Home Base is secure, it will be possible to consider further mutual and balanced troop reductions on both sides of the Iron Curtain. So, assuming that Home Defence will always be required –

whatever reductions in nuclear and conventional forces take place in central Europe – what changes are we likely to see in the Home Defence scene?

One possible way of providing the necessary manpower for Home Defence would be the creation of a so called 'third line' force. Like the Danish Home Guard, it would be the eyes and ears of the field army, relying chiefly on the native skills and local knowledge of its volunteer members. It could not conceivably be regarded as a combat field force and it certainly should not be considered for use in the restoration of law and order if any situation got beyond the control of the police. It would be equipped only so far as is consistent with its role of guarding static installations: rifles of the simplest pattern, pistols, CB type radios, overalls, a respirator and a belt would suffice.

The training of this Home Guard need not impose a heavy load on the Regular and Territorial Armies. There is still a residue of older men who have undertaken some sort of military service who would be able to teach some of the basic military skills. Training assistance from the Army would need to be no more than occasional help from travelling training teams and the provision of some centrally held courses at schools of military instruction. There would be no need for parading or ceremonial and, although on mobilization all ranks would have to be subject to military law, the informality of such a volunteer force would soon find its own level and type of discipline.

Most other European nations can very quickly create a large pool of military manpower since they are national service nations. Within five days of a general mobilization the Swedes – a neutral and unmilitaristic nation tied to no alliances – can mobilize more than ten per cent of their population for the defence of their country: 800,000 men and women are able to take their places in the defence of Sweden within 72 hours and this excludes half a million organized for civil defence.[1] Ten per cent of the population of Britain would amount to 6.5 million defenders, whereas we can muster 100,000. Assuming we continue to eschew national service, and there are many good reasons for so doing, the only real alternative is some form of Home Guard.

If a nationwide Home Guard is considered too expensive by any future government, it would be possible to start modestly with cadres and a skeletal organization. What could be decided now, though, is not to dispose of or sell off obsolete equipment. It could be retained for use by a Home Guard. There is considerable evidence to suggest that such a force would not be expensive. A Committee under the Chairmanship of Admiral of the Fleet Lord Hill-Norton, a former Chief of the Defence Staff, concluded in 1983 that it would cost £17.06 million to equip 100,000 volunteers, £42.67 million to equip 250,000 volunteers and £120.00 million to equip 700,000 volunteers.[2] These capital costs would be spread over the five or six years required to bring a Home Guard up to strength. Running costs would be minimal. The volunteers, like the Danish and Norwegian Home Guards, would receive no pay other than a refund of expenses. After initial training, a volunteer would incur virtually no recurring costs. Hill Norton's committee estimated that a volunteer would cost about £100 a year over a six year period; or about half a penny in every £100 of the annual defence budget.[3] Whatever the accuracy of these estimates, one thing is certain: a Home Guard would be very cheap. But, to be realistic, there is no scope for increasing the defence budget to accommodate a Home Guard. It would only be possible in the light of arms reductions and consequent defence budget savings.

It has been suggested that a Home Guard would duplicate the Home Service Force or have a detrimental effect on TA recruiting. This is unlikely. The HSF is only due to be recruited to a ceiling of 5,000 and it is effectively

Left: The four nation Euro fighter Aircraft (EFA) is due in service in the German, Italian, Spanish and British air forces in the mid-1990s as an air defence fighter. An experimental aircraft (see below) manufactured by British Aerospace has already flown as a testbed for the advanced design characteristics of EFA. The project shows every sign of being a winner.

part of the TA. They did a first class job on 'Brave Defender' and can only be judged a great success, but, due mainly to their limited numbers, they cannot possibly provide a nationwide 'watch and ward' in the same way as a Home Guard. With regard to the effect on the TA, it is impossible to be certain, but it is likely that a Home Guard would attract large numbers of men and women who for very good reasons cannot (or will not) join the TA. TA Centres are relatively few and far between; high standards of physical fitness are required; a considerable minimum of annual days of attendance is required. In short the degree of commitment required may not be possible for many people who, nevertheless, would like to play a part in their country's defence at minimal inconvenience to themselves. In view of past disappointments[4] in trying to raise a Home Guard, it would be wise to go cautiously and in stages. For instance, in the first stage, 100,000 volunteers could be the target. If and when that was successful, the scheme could be expanded.

New equipment that could revolutionize the Home Defence scene is on the horizon. One example is the airship. Airship Industries is currently manufacturing an airship which could be used by the Royal navy in the AEW role or as an offshore patrol ship. For this latter role it is suggested that the craft should operate at altitudes of about 2,000 feet in winds of up to 30 knots. Its cost is said by its designers to compare very favourably with surface vessels, one estimate[5] putting the cost of a fully equipped 12–1500 ton surface ship at £36–40 million and that of an 85,000m^3 airship with both air and surface radar, Vulcan guns port and starboard, dipping sonar and sonobuoys at about £25 million. It would not be as vulnerable as might be imagined. It has a notably low radar signature and a zero IR image for homing missiles. Even though it would be vulnerable to direct aimed fire, in some circumstances it would be more survivable than a ship.

An airship could cover twenty times the area that could be covered by a surface ship in a comparable patrol. Operating at about 35 knots, it could have an endurance of sixteen days, compared to ten days at 18 knots for a typical surface craft, and has the added advantage of a dash capability of about 100 knots if it needs to get to a particular location in a hurry. It would require a crew of only fifteen whereas a conventional patrol ship, for instance the Vosper Thornycroft Offshore Patrol vessel, requires 64 all ranks.[6] The French Navy have already tested a Skyship 600 produced by Airship Industries as have other commercial organizations in Japan, Venezuela, the United Kingdom and elsewhere. It remains to be seen whether or not airships are a viable alternative for Home Defence purposes, but the omens are certainly promising.

In the air, the future of air defence lies with the Eurofighter aircraft or EFA. Like Tornado, this is another collaborative project, on this occasion involving Aeritalia (Italy), British Aerospace (United Kingdom), CASA (Spain) and Messerschmitt-Bölkow Blohm in partnership with Dornier (Germany). More than 800 EFAs are likely to be built under a four nation agreement to meet the common requirement of the air forces of the four nations whose participation in the project is split United Kingdom 33 per cent, West Germany 33 per cent, Italy 21 per cent and Spain 13 per cent. Four of Europe's leading aero engine companies: Fiat Aviazione of Italy, Motoren und Turbinen-Union of Germany, Rolls Royce of Britain and Sener of Spain have formed a new company, Eurojet Turbo GmbH to design, develop, manufacture and support the proposed two spool reheated turbofan engine to be known as theEJ200.

The aircraft will be a canard delta, single seat, twin engined aircraft optimized in the air to air combat role for service from the mid 1990s. Unlike

Right: Airships may well be able to carry out the functions of surface patrol vessels much more efficiently. This photograph shows a Skyship 600 manufactured by Airship Industries on surveillance duties over a North Sea oil rig. Several navies, including the US Navy, are experimenting with airships for patrol duties.

the Tornado, which is primarily designed as an interdiction aircraft but has been adapted for air defence, the EFA will take advantage of all the latest technology to make it the ideal air defence fighter: it will use carbon fibre composites and new lightweight alloys so that its basic mass empty weight will be only 9.75 tonnes with a gross wing area of 50 square metres. It will incorporate 'active control technology' (computer controlled avionics) so as to provide all the performance benefits of a naturally unstable design. And it will be fitted with low drag missile installations to improve aircraft performance, and 'stealth' technology will be built into the aircraft. The radar will have a multi target capability. The EFA promises to be a really first class aircraft and will keep European aircraft manufacturers in the forefront of fighter technology.

It is likely to be armed with ASRAAM or Advanced Short Range Air to Air Missile which is being developed as the key weapon system for the aircraft of the 1990s. Again this is a collaborative project involving mainly British Aerospace but also Bodenseewerk Gerätetechnik, Thorn EMI Electronics,

Messerschmitt Bölkow Blohm, Junghaus and Raufoss and Garrett Canada. It is wingless and highly agile with a highly sensitive infra red seeker that can lock on to its target before launch or in flight giving the missile a fire-and-forget capability.

These are some of the technical improvements on the horizon at sea and in the air. They are for the most part evolutionary rather than revolutionary changes. On land there are unlikely to be any startling developments in the near future. Provided that funds remain available there should be, however, a steady improvement in infantry equipment and – if some form of Home Guard is instituted – of manpower. The three areas in which equipment improvements would be welcome would be surveillance and perimeter protection equipment for the better defence of KPs against attack from the ground; improved and more comprehensive radio communications throughout the entire civil and military Home Defence infrastructure, and some form of defence against attack from the air for some of our key military installations such as early warning sites and naval bases.

The main aims of a perimeter protection system are to provide the earliest possible detection of intruders; to maximize the reaction time for a Quick

Below: An artist's impression of the Eurofighter Aircraft (EFA) firing an ASRAAM.

Reaction Force; to ensure that the system cannot be overcome by tampering; to give a low (preferably negligible) false alarm rate; to ensure reliability over long periods as well as easy installation, and ideally the system should provide protection in depth. All of this is a tall order but the equipment does exist. It would represent considerable capital expenditure and could only be afforded for the most vital KPs.

Perimeter protection can be provided by microwave/IR fences, tripwire/differential force systems, by acoustic, seismic or magnetic sensors, or by radar or TV surveillance. Often a combination of these systems is the best answer. Sensors can provide protection in a number of ways: they can detect an intruder crossing a line, they can detect attempts to climb or interfere with fences or walls, and they can sense interference with windows. Additionally or alternatively, they can be used to provide focal protection so that the presence of a person in a room is indicated. Most perimeter protection systems are connected to a central control or station, thus keeping to a minimum the manpower required to monitor them. Ideally any security system installed should perform the following functions.

- Deter an intruder from entering;
- Detect a security threat before it happens;
- Sense an intrusion when it takes place and pinpoint where it has occurred;
- Locate the intruder so as to determine the nature of the threat; and
- Respond to the threat and neutralize it.

Clearly this latter function is performed by men. But such a system would reduce the overall manpower bill drastically. When manpower is at such a premium, the future defence of KPs must rely to a greater extent on perimeter protection, surveillance devices and intruder alarms.

The most notable trend in Home Defence, however, is likely to be a continuation of the new all hazards approach to Civil Defence. Indeed this trend has already made the more widely understood term of Civil Defence obsolescent and replaced it with Cvil Protection. Disaster can strike in peacetime and wartime. Although peacetime disasters seem to strike less well developed nations with depressing frequency,[7] in Britain natural disasters are usually restricted to the effects of heavy snowfalls, extreme cold, flooding and severe storms. While these are not on the same scale as disasters elsewhere in the world, they can still result in large numbers of people left stranded, or homeless, communications and power supplies disrupted and water and sewage facilities cut off. The east coast floods in 1953 resulted in the evacuation of 13,000 Canvey Islanders in Essex when waves broke down 20ft sea walls, flooding two thirds of the island. Damage to the coastline covered hundreds of square miles from Yorkshire to Kent. Normal communications failed so amateur radio operators gave help to the Emergency Services. More recently, the centre of York was seriously flooded in 1982.

But Britain is not immune from more serious disasters. In 1966 the coal tip at Aberfan in Glamorgan swept down to engulf the village school and seventeen houses, resulting in the deaths of 144 people. The explosion at the chemical works at Flixborough in 1974 was not on the same scale as Bhopal, but it might have been worse: residents of more than 2,000 damaged houses and shops in twenty villages had to fend for themselves for some time before help could reach them. It was this disaster which caused many local authorities to rethink their civil protection plans. And then in December 1988 the ultimate horror at Lockerbie when a fully laden jumbo jet was blown out of the sky on to a small town.

Thus, in response to these disasters, but also because of a lessening of tension between East and West, a new all hazards approach to Civil

Protection has emerged. As Chernobyl showed us all so clearly even nuclear free zones can be contaminated by radioactive particles. This realization will in time depoliticize Civil Protection.

We live in exciting times. It really does seem possible that there will be a continuing lessening of tension between East and West in the years ahead. Multilateral nuclear and conventional disarmament would now appear to be a real possibility. Substantial conventional force reductions in Europe are likely by 1990. Economic pressures are forcing both the Soviet Union and the Western democracies to spend less on defence. However, only the most naïve among us could possibly believe that all the deep seated enmities and historical differences between the Soviet bloc and the democratic countries of the Western Alliance are going to disappear overnight. Nor should we assume that mankind's habit developed over several milleniums of settling differences occasionally by force is suddenly going to stop. Home Defence, particularly conventional Home Defence, will remain a necessity *ad infinitum*.

Every citizen, be he neutralist, pacifist or unilateralist, has an interest in the defence of his homeland. The defences of Britain are by no means perfect and much remains to be done. But matters have been carefully thought through and they have evolved sensibly so that there are now successive layers of conventional defences. We can be reasonably confident that if ever an aggressor – the Soviet Union or anyone else – tried to attack the British Isles he would receive such a powerful rebuff that it would not be worth his while pursuing his intentions. The seas around our shores have stood us in good stead for centuries. May they continue to do so.

Notes:
1. Tony Baldry and Jim Spicer, *Defence Begins at Home*, CPC Publications, London, 1986, p. 24.
2. Ibid.
3. Ibid, p. 25.
4. In 1951 the Home Guard Act attempted to reintroduce the Home Guard at a time when the Korean War was in progress, the Berlin Airlift was a recent memory and the Cold War was at its height. Despite this, the aim of raising 170,000 men in 1,000 cadre battalions was a failure and the new Home Guard was only recruited to 22 per cent of its planned strength.
5. John Reed, 'Coastal Defence: Some Affordable Solutions', article in Armada International, 1/1986, p. 72.
6. Ibid.
7. In January 1989 the government announced that a new ADP system code named PINDAR would be introduced shortly. Its purpose is to gather and collate information and Intelligence from military HQs so as to keep central government briefed on the Home Defence situation. It is to be based on fibre optics cable communications. The intention is to replace the existing vulnerable microwave links. At the same time a fibre optics communications system will link 200 RAF and RN installations. The Army will develop its existing FASTNET system.
8. Abroad one only has to think of Bhopal in India where in 1984 poisonous fumes from a pesticide plant killed and seriously injured many thousands of local residents. Then in 1978 the Mexico City earthquake reduced the city centre to rubble and, during the same year, there was the collapse of the dam at Stava near Calvese in Italy when three hotels and twenty houses were swept away by a 60 foot wall of mud 600 feet wide. Again, in 1985 the Nevado del Ruiz volcano in Colombia erupted: three towns were overwhelmed and an estimated 20,000 people died. In 1986 there was a nuclear explosion in a Soviet nuclear reactor at Chernobyl in the Ukraine. Vast areas of the country were abandoned and parts of Europe as far afield as the United Kingdom were contaminated. More recently the Soviet Union has veen overwhelmed by a series of disasters including the Armenian earthquake disaster and the Trans Siberian Railway gas explosion.

GLOSSARY OF TERMS

■ **Military Home Defence** Military measures to counter internal threat or external aggression. They include:

a. The protection of key points and supporting installations.

b. The protection of ports and anchorages.

c. The protection of other military installations.

d. The maintenance of the lines of communication within the UK.

e. Civil support for military operations.

■ **Civil Defence** Any measure not amounting to actual combat for affording defence against any form of hostile attack by a foreign power or for depriving any form of hostile attack by a foreign power of the whole or part of its effect, whether the measures are taken before, at, or after the time of attack. It includes military support of these measures.

■ **Civil Military Co-operation** Those actions and measures undertaken by civil authorities and service commanders during times of tension and war, for mutual assistance between the government, civil agencies and population on the one hand and the armed forces on the other. It includes all measures undertaken by the armed forces in providing military aid to the civil authorities.

■ **Regional Government** A system of decentralized government based on Home Defence Regions under Regional Commissioners to govern the country internally. It has two stages initiated by:

a. *Dispersal* The time when staff are deployed in the Warning or Conventional War Periods to Regional Government Headquarters to prepare for the introduction of Regional Government.

b. *Decentralization* The moment when a Regional Government becomes effective. This will be either when the Regional Commissioner receives powers from Central Government to govern his Region or when the failure of communications makes the assumption of these powers necessary.

■ **Mobilization**

a. The act of preparing for war or other emergencies through assembling and organizing national resources.

b. The process by which the armed forces or part of them are brought to a state of readiness for war or other national emergency. This includes assembling and organizing personnel, supplies, and *matériel* for active military service (NATO definition).

■ **United Kingdom Warning and Monitoring Organization (UKWMO)** The Home Office-controlled organization which provides warning of air attack (conventional or nuclear), confirms any nuclear strike, warns of the approach of radioactive fallout, supplies Government Headquarters and Home Defence Forces with a scientific assessment of the path and intensity of fallout and provides a post-attack meteorological service.

■ **Ground Defence Area (GDA)** A GDA is that area surrounding a Key Point that has been mutually agreed by the installation commander, Army District commander and through him Police Chief Constable, as tactically important for the defence of that installation. Troops operating within the GDA are under command or operational control of the officer commanding the installation. Troops operating outside the GDA are normally under the command or operational control of the TAOR commander.

- **Composite General Reserve (CGR)** Company-sized units formed by units of the individual training organization (depots, army apprentice colleges, junior leaders regiments, etc.) and made up of the soldiers under training and their instructors.

- **General Support Unit (GSU)** Company-sized unit formed from reservists. There are two types:
  a. GSU (G&L) (Guard and Labour) which form infantry companies for guard duties and other similar tasks.
  b. GSU (Tpt) (Transport) which form transport squadrons.

- **Home Service Forces (HSF)** The most recent addition to the Home Defence forces. Part of the TA, HSF Companies enable people to enlist up to the age of 55 and serve until the age of 60. They have a lesser training liability than the rest of the TA and their main role is to provide guards at key points.

- **Mobile Reaction Forces (MRF)** A force between Section (8 men) and Platoon (30 men) strength which can deploy rapidly in its own organic transport to form a base location at the scene of an incident, such as an attack on a KP.

- **Tactical Area of Responsibility (TAOR)** A defined area of land in which operational responsibilities are specifically assigned to the military commander of the area for the conduct of tactical operations involving resources under his command or operational control. TAORs correspond, where possible, with Local Authority and Police Force Boundaries. TAOR HQs will be introduced in the Warning Period and revert to being known as County Military Headquarters on Decentralization.

- **Zone Headquarters (ZHQ)** The protected headquarters within Regions. One would be nominated for the use of the Regional Commissioner and called the RHQ; the other ZHQ would be used by his deputy, the DRC.

- **Armed Forces Headquarters (AFHQ)** The protected wartime Joint Service HQ at Regional level.

- **Regional Military Commander (RMC)** An officer designated in peacetime to become, on decentralization, responsible to the Regional Commissioner for the employment of the armed forces under his command.

- **Regional Police Commander (RPC)** A chief police officer designated in peacetime to assume command, on decentralization, of all civil police forces within the region.

- **District War Headquarters** The wartime headquarters of the Army District. This will normally be the same location as the AFHQ.

- **County Emergency Centre (CEC)** The headquarters of the county authority. The equivalent in London are Group Wartime Headquarters.

■ **County Controller** The designated head of the CEC, usually the Chief Executive of the County Authority.

■ **County Military Headquarters (CMHQ)** The military headquarters which parallels the CEC. It may be collocated with the CEC, but where this is not the case an appropriate military representation will be with the CEC. The TAOR HQ becomes the CMHQ on decentralization.

■ **County Military Commander** The military commander who assumes operational control of the Home Defence forces assigned to the county except those previously committed to continuing or pre-planned operations of national or NATO concern. In most cases he will have been the TAOR commander during the Warning and Conventional War Periods.

Index